Slow Cooker Recipes 2021

The Ultimate Slow Cooker Cookbook for Beginners with Easy & Healthy Recipes that the Whole Family Can Enjoy. (Stews, Soups, Casseroles, Risottos, Pilafs & Vegetarian Dishes)

Author: Olivia Parker

Table of Contents

Fundamentals of Slow Cooking – Everything You Need To Know

You may be wondering how a slow cooker works, and why people rave about these gadgets, so let's briefly cover a few of the fundamentals.

What Is A Slow Cooker?

A slow cooker is a large vessel that you cook full meals in. Usually, it is comprised of a heating element, a heavy, insulated vessel that gets heated, and a glass lid that allows you to see into the pot but traps the heat inside.

The heating element heats the vessel from the bottom, and heat spreads upward through the food. Instead of heating the food to boiling very quickly, like a traditional oven or cooker, the slow cooker maintains a low temperature for a long time.

Usually, slow cookers have temperature settings between 175 degrees F and 215 degrees F. You'll pick between low, medium, and high, according to the speed you wish to achieve and the kind of food that you are making.

What Are The Advantages Of A Slow Cooker?

There are a few major advantages to using a slow cooker, but one of the biggest ones is that you can set a meal going in the morning, and it will be ready to eat when you walk back into the house in the evening. That means you can put a pan of soup on before you leave for work, and it will happily bubble away all day, providing you with a delicious, steaming hot meal to come home to.

You won't need to do piles of cleaning up, either, because only the slow cooker dish and the bowls or plates you use to eat the meal will be dirty – everything else will already have been dealt with. Instead of coming home and having to wash, peel, and chop vegetables to cook a whole meal, you can walk in the door and find it waiting for you.

Many people find this enormously appealing, because they don't have to find the energy to cook at the end of a long day at work; it's all done for them.

Secondly, the slow cooker uses considerably less energy than cooking on a stove does. This is because it never needs to achieve a very high heat, and the insulated pot massively increases the efficiency of the cooker by trapping the heat that's transferred to it. A slow cooker can stay hot for hours, even when switched off, because the vessel is so well insulated.

Furthermore, slow cookers are great for making tough cuts of meat deliciously tender. You can buy the cheaper, chewier cuts from the store, and the slow cooker will transform them into delicious, tempting mouthfuls. These cuts would otherwise take a long time to prepare and cook, and would probably cost you extra in terms of energy – which isn't ideal if you are on a budget.

All in all, the slow cooker offers some major advantages, especially to a working professional who is out of the house for around eight or nine hours at a time. You would never leave your stove on, but a slow cooker is safe, energy efficient, and enormously convenient.

Why are Slow Cooker Meals so Effective with Weight Loss?

One of the other major attractions of slow cookers is that they help people to lose weight, and this is because it's easy to make delicious recipes that do not contain a lot of fat. Creating soups and stews becomes wonderfully straightforward, and they will taste fabulous because these kinds of foods benefit from being cooked very slowly. It allows time for the flavors to meld, and allows the spices and herbs to soak into the vegetables and meat.

Furthermore, most slow cooker recipes do not depend on large amounts of oil, because there is usually plenty of liquid involved and the ingredients won't be getting hot enough to risk burning them onto the pan. You will find that most recipes still include some fat, but it's easy to get away with small quantities, rather than needing thick layers of grease in order to make good food.

Of course, you do have to choose healthy options, even with a slow cooker. It does not magically make all foods healthy, so you must make responsible choices – but this tends to be easier to do. Slow cookers are a great way to increase your vegetable intake, because instead of having to boil, roast, steam, stew, sautee, or fry them, you can just toss everything in together and wait for them to cook. Some recipes might encourage you to fry the onions first for a little extra flavor, but on the whole, having a slow cooker massively simplifies your recipes, and lets you put everything in together.

If you don't fancy that, you can always add a little steamed broccoli or a few carrots on the side once the main meal is cooked, so you're not just eating everything mixed in, but this is a sure way to make vegetables a bigger part of your diet – which will certainly aid you in the weight loss journey.

Another big reason that people find slow cookers help them lose weight is that they can make takeaways less attractive. A lot of takeaway meals include things like pizzas, fries, chicken wings, and other fatty, high-carb foods that are not good for your waistline, but the simple fact is that they are convenient and when you don't want to whip up a meal after work, a takeaway often becomes irresistible.

With a slow cooker, however, you'll come home to a hot meal already waiting. This makes it so much easier to resist the temptation than if you have to cook. You can also batch cook, since it's almost as quick to make a double portion. This means you can put some single-portion meals in your freezer, perfect for future dinners. All you need to do is let one defrost in the fridge during the day, or even just stick it in the microwave for ten minutes when you get home, and your dinner is ready. In some ways, it's even easier than ordering a takeaway, and it's definitely cheaper and healthier.

Proven Tips for Weight Loss and How To Keep it Off

Although exercise is certainly an important part of staying healthy and keeping your weight down, most people are aware that weight is far more about what you put into your body than what you do with it. That means healthy eating is crucial, but how do you keep this up in the long term, and how can your slow cooker help?

Tip One: Build Habits

A lot of people struggle with sustained weight loss, even if they can manage temporary weight loss, and you might be wondering why. One of the key factors is that when you first start a new diet, you've got the motivation to make big sacrifices – but you can't do this in the long term if you don't build habits around them. You will find yourself slipping back into old ways.

It's easy to commit to cooking yourself a healthy, from-scratch meal every day after work, and you might stick at this for a few weeks, or a couple of months, but then a harder day comes up, or you're particularly tired, or you want to reward yourself, and the takeout menus or microwave meals creep back into your life. That's because you've made dieting harder, not easier, so you inevitably fall back to old habits when your motivation starts to wane.

A slow cooker, however, makes your new habit far more sustainable, because it makes your life easier. There's a lot of satisfaction in coming home to a freshly cooked, piping hot meal that is the result of hard work and good organization – but it doesn't demand anything of you at the end of a long, busy day. You shift the effort aspect to a time when you are not tired or busy, and you also reduce it by making the cooking simpler.

Tip Two: Eat More Vegetables

Furthermore, although you do need to think about what you are putting into your slow cooker, there is a high chance that your diet will start to incorporate more vegetables, simply because these are a major part of many slow cooker recipes and you will therefore get into the habit of eating them.

This will encourage you to eat them more even when you aren't using your slow cooker, since we tend to like the foods that we eat, and we're more likely to crave these things – so they will creep into other aspects of your diet too. Slow cookers make vegetables delicious and easy, so they are a great way to push your overall diet in a healthier direction.

Tip Three: Eat More Whole Grains And Legumes

One of the biggest challenges many people face when it comes to diet is feeling hungry all the time, because they're changing what they are eating. This makes it really hard to sustain the diet; it's okay to be hungry for a while, but being perpetually hungry is exhausting and unpleasant.

The answer to this is to eat more whole grains, such as brown rice, but the issue with whole grains is that they can be a fiddle to cook. Lentils, beans, whole grain rice, and dried peas are high fiber foods that will make you feel full and satisfied by your main meal, but they tend to be a bit more of a challenge to cook – namely because they take longer, so you're less likely to have the energy for them in the evenings. By tossing them in the slow cooker, you make it considerably easier to include these foods in your diet regularly. This should reduce any hunger pangs, making your diet more sustainable.

Other Tips

Of course, there are many other elements to achieving sustained weight loss, and a slow cooker is not going to help with all of them. Things you should look to be doing include:

- Planning your meals; a slow cooker may or may not help with this one, but a lot of people do incorporate meal planning when they start to use a slow cooker, because it does require a bit of forethought. You can't throw something quick in your slow cooker, so having an idea about what you're going to make in advance is helpful – and this will help you to look at your diet as a whole and work out whether it is healthy and sustainable. It will encourage more introspection on the things that you eat and whether they are balanced and healthy.

- Avoiding junk food; if you feel fuller as a result of eating more filling foods (wholegrain rice, etc.), you are less likely to start craving junk food later on in the evening, and this may help you to make healthier choices overall. Again, we crave the things that we eat a lot, so it may take a while for sugar cravings or pizza cravings to go away, but being satisfied by your evening meal should help.

- Eating regularly; if you get into the habit of setting your slow cooker every day before you go to work, you'll soon find that your evening meal becomes regulated, and you aren't tempted to add a whole bunch of sides (which could happen when ordering a takeout after work) or a huge dessert.

4 Mistakes You Must Avoid

Like learning to use any new gadget, there are a few things you will quickly learn not to do with your slow cooker – but here are some of the top ones, so you can be ahead of the game and avoid making them entirely.

Mistake One: Not Defrosting Your Meat

This is a big "no" when it comes to using your slow cooker, even if it might seem harmless. It can be hard to approach meals with good organization to begin with, and if you've forgotten to thaw some meat in advance, you might be tempted to just toss it into the slow cooker frozen. After all, the heat will soon defrost it, right? You may even have done this when making soup or stew on the stove, and it's always been fine.

Unfortunately, this is not a safe approach with a slow cooker meal. The slow cooker's temperature increases very gradually, which will mean that the meat stays in the "danger zone" that allows bacteria to multiply quickly for far longer than is considered safe. Some people even find that the meat is still raw or frozen in the center, even when the outside is thoroughly cooked and ready to eat.

If you need to defrost meat quickly, use the microwave or cold water (not hot water) before adding it to your slow cooker. Do not put frozen or partially thawed meat into the slow cooker; you run a high risk of giving yourself food poisoning.

Mistake Two: Not Preparing Vegetables Properly

Although you probably want to make slow cooking as simple as possible, it is true that just tossing all the vegetables in at once can make your dish less appetizing, because they will have different cook times. Some recipes will allow for this behavior, so if you're going to be at work all day, look out for ones that don't require staggered ingredient additions – but on the whole, recipes will work better if you add soft ingredients later.

This doesn't mean a slow cooker can never work for you. You may find that you can quickly toss in a handful of ingredients when you get in from work, allow the pot another twenty minutes of simmering, and then serve a delicious meal with no mushy ingredients. An example of this would be mushrooms or peas. Both of these will start to break down if they are simmered for eight hours straight, which can lead to a mushy, unappetizing meal. Adding them about twenty minutes or half an hour before you want to serve the dish will make a big difference.

If you really don't want to do this, there are recipes that allow you to add all the ingredients at once because they have a similar cook time, so simply look out for these. However, if a recipe tells you to sautee an ingredient first or add it later, it's a good idea to pay attention if you want a fantastic result.

Mistake Three: Adding Too Much Water

You might feel like the slow cooker is going to need a lot of liquid if it can safely be simmered for an entire day, and consequently add plenty of extra stock. However, this is something to be wary of. Your slow cooker actually won't need significant amounts of water, because the lid will trap almost all of the steam in, and it will drip back down onto the meal. Little water is lost throughout the cooking process, except when you remove the lid, so don't add lots of water to begin with.

Mistake Four: Using Tender Meats

You might think that better cuts will produce the best meals, whether cooked on the stove or in the slow cooker, but this is simply not the case. Tender, expensive meats can be ruined by a slow cooker, because they will turn mushy and fall apart.

You should choose tougher, cheaper cuts for your slow cooker meals, and save any luxury ones for the grill or the stove.

Soup Recipes

Tomato Soup

Servings|6   Time|6 hours 40 minutes

Nutritional Content (per serving):

Cal| 333   Fat| 27.2g   Protein| 9.6g   Carbs| 16.3g

Ingredients:

- 15 millilitres olive oil
- 100 grams celery, chopped finely
- 120 grams onions, chopped finely
- 20 grams fresh basil, chopped
- 1 bay leaf
- 15 grams whole-wheat flour
- 435 millilitres warm coconut milk
- 150 grams carrots, peeled and chopped finely
- 1 (680-grams) can whole plum tomatoes, crushed with juice
- 1140 millilitres chicken broth
- Salt and ground black pepper, as required
- 40 grams Pecorino Romano cheese, grated

Directions:

1. In a non-stick skillet, heat olive oil over medium heat and cook carrots, celery and onion, for about 5-6 minutes.
2. Transfer the onion mixture into a slow cooker.
3. Add tomatoes, basil, broth, bay leaf and black pepper and mix well.
4. Set the slow cooker on "Low" and cook, covered for 6 hours.
5. Uncover the slow cooker and let the soup cool slightly.
6. Transfer the soup into a blender in batches and pulse until smooth.
7. Transfer soup into a pan over low heat.
8. In a small pan, melt butter over low heat and cook flour and cook for about 1-2 minutes, stirring continuously.
9. Add in 1240 millilitres of hot soup and stir to combine.
10. Stir in warm milk and transfer the flour mixture into the soup with cheese.
11. Cook for about 10-15 minutes, stirring occasionally.
12. Serve hot.

Onion Soup

Servings|6   Time|5 hours 25 minutes

Nutritional Content (per serving):

Cal| 112   Fat| 7.1g   Protein| 7g   Carbs| 6g

Ingredients:

- 30 millilitres olive oil
- 2 garlic cloves, minced
- 5 grams unsweetened applesauce
- 5 grams dried basil, crushed
- 1200 millilitres vegetable broth
- 30 grams Parmesan cheese, grated
- 2 medium sweet onions, sliced
- 60 millilitres low-sodium soy sauce
- 5 grams dried oregano, crushed
- Salt and ground black pepper, as required

Directions:

1. In a skillet, heat oil over medium heat and cook the onion for about 8-9 minutes, stirring frequently.
2. Add garlic and cook for about 1 minute.
3. Transfer the onion mixture into a slow cooker.
4. Add remaining ingredients except for cheese and mix well.
5. Set the slow cooker on "Low" and cook, covered for 4-5 hours.
6. Uncover and immediately stir in cheese until melted completely.
7. Serve hot.

Creamy Broccoli Soup

Servings|6   Time|6 hours 25 minutes

Nutritional Content (per serving):

Cal| 238   Fat| 20.4g   Protein| 6.9g   Carbs| 8.4g

Ingredients:

- ❖ 30 grams butter
- ❖ 2 garlic cloves, minced
- ❖ 360 grams small broccoli florets
- ❖ Salt and ground black pepper, as required

- ❖ 1 onion, chopped
- ❖ 5 grams rosemary, chopped
- ❖ 1200 millilitres vegetable broth
- ❖ 240 grams heavy cream

Directions:

1. In a skillet, melt butter over medium heat and sauté onion for about 3-4 minutes.
2. Add garlic and rosemary and sauté for about 1 minute.
3. Transfer the onion mixture into a slow cooker and stir in broccoli, broth and black pepper.
4. Set the slow cooker on "Low" and cook, covered for 6 hours.
5. Uncover the slow cooker and let the soup cool slightly.
6. Transfer the soup into a blender and pulse until smooth.
7. Now transfer the soup into a pan over medium heat and stir in cream.
8. Cook for about 4-5 minutes, stirring frequently.
9. Serve hot.

Cauliflower & Leek Soup

Servings|4   Time|4 hours 10 minutes

Nutritional Content (per serving):

Cal| 100   Fat| 1.7g   Protein| 7.5g   Carbs| 14.7g

Ingredients:

- ❖ 3 leeks, cut into 1-inch pieces
- ❖ 3 garlic cloves, chopped finely
- ❖ 960 millilitres vegetable broth
- ❖ 10 grams fresh basil
- ❖ 1 large cauliflower head, chopped
- ❖ Salt and ground black pepper as required

Directions:

1. In a slow cooker, add all the ingredients and mix well.
2. Set the slow cooker on "High" and cook, covered for 3-4 hours.
3. Uncover the slow cooker and with an immersion blender, blend until smooth.
4. Serve hot.

Cabbage Soup

Servings|6   Time|4¼ hours

Nutritional Content (per serving):

Cal| 93   Fat| 1.3g   Protein| 6.2g   Carbs| 16.1g

Ingredients:

- 500 grams cabbage, shredded
- 3 carrots, peeled and chopped
- 1 onion, chopped
- 450 grams tomato sauce
- 5 grams dried parsley
- Salt and ground black pepper, as required
- 100 grams tomatoes, chopped finely
- 4-5 garlic cloves, minced
- 960-1200 millilitres vegetable broth
- 5 grams dried oregano

Directions:

1. In a slow cooker, add all ingredients and stir to combine.
2. Set the slow cooker on "High" and cook, covered for 3-4 hours.
3. Serve hot.

Squash & Apple Soup

Servings|6   Time|8¼ hours

Nutritional Content (per serving):

Cal| 134   Fat| 1.4g   Protein| 3.8g   Carbs| 30.3g

Ingredients:

- ❖ 840 grams butternut squash, peeled and chopped
- ❖ 1 large carrot, peeled and chopped
- ❖ 480 millilitres chicken broth
- ❖ Salt and ground black pepper, as required
- ❖ 2 medium apples, peeled, cored and chopped
- ❖ 1 small onion, chopped
- ❖ 1 garlic clove, minced
- ❖ 5 grams dried oregano, crushed
- ❖ 240 millilitres hot unsweetened almond milk

Directions:

1. In a slow cooker, add all ingredients except for almond milk and stir to combine.
2. Set the slow cooker on "Low" and cook, covered for 6-8 hours.
3. Uncover and stir in the almond milk.
4. Uncover the slow cooker and with an immersion blender, blend until smooth.
5. Serve hot.

Spiced Veggie Soup

Servings|6   Time|8 hours

Nutritional Content (per serving):

Cal| 182   Fat| 6.3g   Protein| 9.5g   Carbs| 25.8g

Ingredients:

- 1 medium onion, sliced
- 350 grams green olives, pitted and sliced
- 4 tomatoes, chopped
- 300 grams tomato paste
- 5 grams ground cumin
- 5 grams cayenne pepper
- Salt and ground black pepper, as required
- 2 garlic cloves, minced
- 4 carrots, peeled and sliced
- 1 green capsicum, seeded and sliced
- 1 green chili, chopped
- 5 grams ground coriander
- 5 grams dried oregano
- 1440 millilitres vegetable broth

Directions:

1. In a slow cooker, add all ingredients and mix well.
2. Set the slow cooker on "Low" and cook, covered for 7-8 hours.
3. Serve hot.

Mixed Veggie Soup

Servings|6   Time|8 hours 20 minutes

Nutritional Content (per serving):

Cal| 80   Fat| 3.6g   Protein| 4.9g   Carbs| 8g

Ingredients:

- 15 millilitres olive oil
- 1 celery stalk, chopped
- 2 garlic cloves, minced
- 5 grams dried oregano, crushed
- 2 tomatoes, chopped
- 960 millilitres vegetable broth
- 1 onion, chopped
- 1 large carrot, peeled and chopped
- 1 large courgette, chopped
- 30 grams fresh spinach, chopped
- Salt and ground black pepper as required

Directions:

1. In a skillet, heat the oil over medium heat and sauté onion, celery and carrot for about 3-4 minutes.
2. Add garlic and thyme and sauté for about 1 minute.
3. Transfer the onion mixture into a slow cooker.
4. Add the remaining ingredients and stir to combine.
5. Set the slow cooker on "Low" and cook, covered for 6-8 hours.
6. Serve hot.

Beans & Potato Soup

Servings|6   Time|8¼ hours

Nutritional Content (per serving):

Cal| 193   Fat| 5.2g   Protein| 9.2g   Carbs| 31.8g

Ingredients:

- 15 millilitres olive oil
- 1 potato, cut into cubes
- 240 millilitres tomato juice
- 600 millilitres vegetable broth
- 65 grams red pepper flakes, crushed
- Salt and ground black pepper, as required
- 1 onion, chopped
- 1 (425-gram) can Great Northern beans
- 170 grams sweet potato puree
- Pinch of ground allspice
- 2½ grams paprika
- 10 grams curry powder

Directions:

1. In a skillet, heat olive oil over medium heat and sauté for onion 3-5 minutes.
2. Transfer the onion into a slow cooker.
3. Add the remaining ingredients and stir to combine.
4. Add in potato, beans, tomato juice, vegetable broth, potato puree, coconut milk, red pepper flakes, black pepper, allspice, paprika, curry powder and sea salt and mix well.
5. Set the slow cooker on "Low" and cook, covered for 6-8 hours.
6. Serve hot.

Barley & Beans Soup

Servings|10   Time|8½ hours

Nutritional Content (per serving):

Cal| 149   Fat| 4g   Protein| 6.8g   Carbs| 23.3g

Ingredients:

- ❖ 180 grams dried Great Northern beans, rinsed
- ❖ 1 small onion, chopped
- ❖ 4 garlic cloves, minced
- ❖ 10 grams mixed dried herbs, crushed
- ❖ Salt and ground black pepper, as required
- ❖ 30 millilitres olive oil
- ❖ 100 grams pearl barley
- ❖ 2 medium carrots, peeled and chopped
- ❖ 2 celery stalks, chopped
- ❖ 1 (395-gram) can whole tomatoes with liquid, chopped
- ❖ 1440 millilitres water
- ❖ 90 grams fresh spinach, chopped
- ❖ 30 grams Parmesan cheese, grated

Directions:

1. In a slow cooker, add all ingredients except for spinach and oil and stir to combine.
2. Set the slow cooker on "High" and cook, covered for 8 hours.
3. Uncover the slow cooker and stir in cheese and spinach.
4. Cook, uncovered for 10-15 minutes.
5. Serve hot with the drizzling of oil.

Lentil & Veggie Soup

Servings|12   Time|9 hours 10 minutes

Nutritional Content (per serving):

Cal| 194   Fat| 3.8g   Protein| 12.7g   Carbs| 28.4g

Ingredients:

- ❖ 30 millilitres olive oil
- ❖ 300 grams celery, chopped finely
- ❖ 4 garlic cloves, minced
- ❖ 5 grams ground cumin
- ❖ 1¼ grams ground cinnamon
- ❖ 300 grams cauliflower, chopped
- ❖ 800 grams canned diced tomatoes
- ❖ 1440 millilitres vegetable broth
- ❖ 120 grams fresh spinach, chopped
- ❖ 360 grams onions, chopped finely
- ❖ 5 grams ground coriander
- ❖ 5 grams ground turmeric
- ❖ Salt and ground black pepper, as required
- ❖ 370 grams lentils
- ❖ 40 grams tomato paste
- ❖ 480 millilitres water
- ❖ 40 grams fresh coriander, chopped

Directions:

1. In a large skillet, heat oil over medium heat and sauté onion and celery for about 8-9 minutes.
2. Add garlic and spices and sauté for about 1 minute more.
3. Transfer the onion mixture into a slow cooker.
4. Add remaining ingredients except for spinach and coriander and stir to combine.
5. Set the slow cooker on "Low" and cook, covered for 8-8½ hours.
6. Uncover the slow cooker and stir in spinach.
7. Set the slow cooker on "High" and cook, covered for 30 minutes.
8. Serve hot with the garnishing of coriander.

Chicken & Kale Soup

Servings|6   Time|6¼ hours

Nutritional Content (per serving):

Cal| 222   Fat| 6.3g   Protein| 31g   Carbs| 8.8g

Ingredients:

- ❖ 500 grams cooked chicken, shredded
- ❖ 1 medium onion, chopped finely
- ❖ Salt and ground black pepper, as required
- ❖ 15 millilitres fresh lemon juice
- ❖ 330 grams fresh kale, tough ribs removed and chopped
- ❖ 2 garlic cloves, minced
- ❖ 15 millilitres olive oil
- ❖ 1440 millilitre chicken broth

Directions:

1. In a slow cooker, add all ingredients except for lemon juice and stir to combine.
2. Set the slow cooker on "Low" and cook, covered for 6 hours.
3. Uncover the slow cooker and stir in lemon juice.
4. Serve hot.

Chicken & Rice Soup

Servings|10   Time|9¼ hours

Nutritional Content (per serving):

Cal| 280   Fat| 12.4g   Protein| 27.9g   Carbs| 14.2g

Ingredients:

- 910 grams bone-in chicken breasts
- 3 carrots, peeled and chopped
- 2 (910-millilitre) boxes chicken broth
- 400 millilitres unsweetened coconut milk
- 1 onion, chopped
- 3 celery stalks, chopped
- 15 grams curry powder
- 95 grams long-grain brown rice
- 40 grams fresh coriander, chopped

Directions:

1. In a slow cooker, place chicken and top with vegetables, curry powder and broth.
2. Set the slow cooker on "Low" and cook, covered for 7-8 hours.
3. Uncover the slow cooker and transfer chicken breasts onto a plate.
4. Remove meat from bones and then chop it.
5. In the slow cooker, add the chopped meat, rice and coconut milk and stir to combine.
6. Set the slow cooker on "Low" and cook, covered for 40-60 minutes.
7. Garnish with coriander and serve hot.

Chicken & Corn Soup

Servings|6   Time|9¼ hours

Nutritional Content (per serving):

Cal| 408   Fat| 4.9g   Protein| 38g   Carbs| 57.6g

Ingredients:

- ❖ 910 grams chicken breast, cubed
- ❖ 3 (480-gram) cans creamed corn
- ❖ 2 celery stalks, chopped
- ❖ Salt and ground black pepper, as required
- ❖ 1 onion, chopped
- ❖ 115 grams tomato sauce
- ❖ 2 potatoes, cubed
- ❖ 1920 millilitres water

Directions:

1. In a slow cooker, add all ingredients and mix well.
2. Set the slow cooker on "Low" and cook, covered for 8-9 hours.
3. Serve hot.

Chicken & Spaghetti Soup

Servings|8   Time|8¼ hours

Nutritional Content (per serving):

Cal| 201   Fat| 4.3g   Protein| 27.6g   Carbs| 13g

Ingredients:

- 910 grams skinless, boneless chicken breast, cubed
- 100 grams celery, chopped
- 2 garlic cloves, minced
- 225 grams whole wheat spaghetti, broken
- 1 large onion, chopped
- 4 carrots, peeled and chopped
- 20 grams parsley, chopped
- Salt and ground black pepper, as required
- 1440 millilitres water

Directions:

1. In a slow cooker, mix together all ingredients except for spaghetti.
2. Set the slow cooker on "Low" and cook, covered for 6-7 hours.
3. Uncover the slow cooker and stir in spaghetti.
4. Set the slow cooker on "Low" and cook, covered for 1 hour.
5. Serve hot.

Beef & Potato Soup

Servings|8   Time|8¼ hours

Nutritional Content (per serving):

Cal| 528   Fat| 43.5g   Protein| 21.4g   Carbs| 11.7g

Ingredients:

- ❖ 1440 millilitres vegetable broth, divided
- ❖ 2 garlic cloves, minced
- ❖ 1 medium sweet potato, peeled and chopped
- ❖ 2 celery stalks, chopped
- ❖ Salt and ground black pepper, as required
- ❖ 680 grams cherry tomatoes, halved
- ❖ 25 grams Italian seasoning
- ❖ 2 carrots, peeled and chopped
- ❖ 1 bulb fennel, sliced
- ❖ 910 grams lean boneless beef, cubed
- ❖ 1 bay leaf

Directions:

1. In a blender, add 480 millilitres of broth, tomatoes, garlic and seasoning and pulse until smooth.
2. Add vegetables in a slow cooker and place beef on top.
3. Now, add tomato sauce and remaining broth.
4. Set the slow cooker on "Low" and cook, covered for 6-8 hours.
5. Serve hot.

Meatballs & Courgette Soup

Servings|10   Time|6½ hours

Nutritional Content (per serving):

Cal| 268   Fat| 11.4g   Protein| 34.6g   Carbs| 6g

Ingredients:

For Meatballs

- 910 grams lean ground beef
- 2 garlic cloves, minced
- 20 grams parsley leaves, chopped
- 55 grams Parmesan cheese, grated
- 1 egg, beaten
- 5 grams dried oregano, crushed
- 5 grams dried rosemary, crushed
- Salt and ground black pepper, as required
- 30 millilitres olive oil

For Soup

- 1 medium celery stalk, chopped
- 1 small onion, chopped
- 1 small carrot, peeled and chopped
- 2 medium tomatoes, chopped finely
- 3 large courgettes, spiralized with blade C
- Salt and ground black pepper, as required
- 1680 millilitres beef broth

Directions:

1. For meatballs: in a bowl, add all ingredients and mix until well combined.
2. Make small equal-sized balls from mixture.
3. In a large skillet, heat oil over medium-high heat and cook meatballs in 2 batches for about 4-5 minutes or until golden brown from all sides.
4. In a slow cooker, add celery, onion, carrot and tomato and top with courgette noodles.
5. Sprinkle with salt and black pepper and top with broth.
6. Carefully place the meatballs in the slow cooker.
7. Set the slow cooker on "Low" and cook, covered for 6 hours.
8. Serve hot with the garnishing of parsley.

Ham Soup

Servings|8   Time|8 hours 25 minutes

Nutritional Content (per serving):

Cal| 463   Fat| 21.4g   Protein| 42.6g   Carbs| 21.9g

Ingredients:

- 30 millilitres olive oil
- 5 grams fresh ginger, grated
- 1 yellow capsicum, chopped
- 5 grams fresh thyme, chopped
- Salt and ground black pepper, as required
- 20 grams fresh parsley, chopped
- 1 medium onion, sliced
- 4 celery stalks, chopped
- 70 grams potatoes, chopped
- 225 grams split green peas
- 910 grams smoked ham hocks
- 1440 millilitres vegetable broth

Directions:

1. In a skillet, heat oil over medium heat and cook onion, garlic, ginger, capsicum, celery, potatoes, thyme, split green peas, salt and pepper for about 10 minutes, stirring occasionally.
2. Transfer to the slow cooker.
3. Add vegetable broth and smoked ham hocks and mix well.
4. Set the slow cooker on "Low" and cook, covered for 7-8 hours.
5. Uncover the slow cooker and stir in parsley.
6. Serve hot.

Sausage & Beans Soup

Servings|8   Time|6¼ hours

Nutritional Content (per serving):

Cal| 251   Fat| 17.1g   Protein| 15.5g   Carbs| 9.2g

Ingredients:

- ❖ 455 grams smoked turkey sausage
- ❖ 1 onion, chopped
- ❖ 1 garlic clove, minced
- ❖ 960 millilitres chicken broth
- ❖ Salt and ground black pepper, as required

- ❖ 455 grams mixed dry beans, rinsed, soaked overnight and drained
- ❖ 1 (680-gram) can diced tomatoes with liquid

Directions:

1. In a slow cooker, add all ingredients and stir to combine.
2. Set the slow cooker on "High" and cook, covered for 5-6 hours.
3. Serve hot.

Bacon & Potato Soup

Servings|8   Time|8 ½ hours

Nutritional Content (per serving):

Cal| 539   Fat| 26.3g   Protein| 19.8g   Carbs| 59.6g

Ingredients:

- 15 millilitres olive oil
- 4 carrots, peeled and chopped
- 1 medium onion, sliced
- 2 jalapeño peppers, seeded and chopped
- 1365 grams baking potatoes, peeled and sliced
- 500 millilitres unsweetened coconut milk
- 240 grams heavy cream
- 4 bacon slices, chopped
- 4 celery stalks, chopped
- 2 garlic cloves, minced
- 1¼ grams cayenne pepper
- Salt and ground black pepper, as required
- 1440 millilitres chicken broth
- 115 grams cheddar cheese, shredded
- 20 grams fresh parsley, chopped

Directions:

1. In a skillet, heat oil over medium heat and cook bacon for about 4-5 minutes.
2. Add carrot, celery, onion, garlic, jalapeño peppers, cayenne pepper, salt and black pepper and cook for about 5 minutes.
3. Transfer the bacon mixture into a slow cooker.
4. Add potatoes, chicken broth and coconut milk and mix well.
5. Set the slow cooker on "Low" and cook, covered for 7-8 hours.
6. Uncover the slow cooker and let the soup cool slightly.
7. Transfer the soup into a blender in batches and pulse until smooth.
8. Transfer the soup into a large pan and stir in cheese and cream.
9. Cook for about 4-5 minutes, stirring frequently.
10. Garnish with parsley and serve hot.

Seafood & Spinach Soup

Servings|8   Time|2½ hours

Nutritional Content (per serving):

Cal| 417   Fat| 17.1g   Protein| 53.9g   Carbs| 11.2g

Ingredients:

- 1440 millilitres chicken broth
- 1 medium onion, chopped
- 50 grams celery stalk, chopped
- 180 grams fresh spinach, chopped
- 50 grams fresh parsley, chopped
- Salt and ground black pepper, as required
- 455 grams large shrimp, peeled and deveined
- 25 grams green onions, chopped
- 45 millilitres olive oil
- 75 grams carrot, peeled and chopped
- 200 grams tomatoes, chopped finely
- 5 grams garlic powder
- 910 grams salmon fillets, cubed
- 910 grams sea mussels, beards removed and scrubbed
- 15 grams fresh lime juice

Directions:

1. In a slow cooker, add all ingredients except for seafood, lime juice and green onion.
2. Set the slow cooker on "High" and cook, covered for 1¾ hours.
3. Uncover the slow cooker and place salmon over vegetable mixture, followed by scallops over mussels and shrimps.
4. Set the slow cooker on "High" and cook, covered for 35-45 minutes.
5. Uncover and stir in lime juice.
6. Serve with the topping of green onion.

Stew Recipes

Mixed Veggie Stew

Servings|6   Time|6¼ hours

Nutritional Content (per serving):

Cal| 137   Fat| 7g   Protein| 5.9g   Carbs| 15.3g

Ingredients:

- ❖ 30 millilitres extra-virgin olive oil
- ❖ 1 small brinjal, chopped
- ❖ 70 grams Kalamata olives, pitted and chopped
- ❖ 960 millilitres vegetable broth
- ❖ 2½ grams dried parsley
- ❖ 5 grams red pepper flakes, crushed
- ❖ 20 grams fresh chives, minced

- ❖ 4 garlic cloves, chopped
- ❖ 1 medium onion, chopped
- ❖ 1 medium capsicum, seeded and chopped
- ❖ 2 (425-gram) cans diced tomatoes
- ❖ 2½ grams dried oregano
- ❖ Salt and ground black pepper, as required

Directions:

1. In a slow cooker, place all the ingredients except for chives and stir to combine.
2. Set the slow cooker on "Low" and cook, covered for 4-6 hours.
3. Serve hot with the garnishing of chives.

Chickpeas & Kale Stew

Servings|6   Time|7¾ hours

Nutritional Content (per serving):

Cal| 238   Fat| 3.3g   Protein| 8.9g   Carbs| 35.1g

Ingredients:

- 2 (400-gram) cans fire-roasted diced tomatoes
- 4 garlic cloves, minced
- 2½ grams red pepper flakes, crushed
- 720 millilitres vegetable broth
- 440 grams fresh kale, tough ribs removed and chopped
- 45 millilitres olive oil
- 100 grams carrot, peeled and chopped
- 5 grams dried oregano
- Salt and ground black pepper, as required
- 1 (425-gram) can chickpeas, rinsed, drained and divided
- 15 millilitres fresh lemon juice

Directions:

1. In a slow cooker, place the tomatoes, onion, carrot, garlic, oregano, red pepper flakes, salt, black pepper and broth and stir to combine.
2. Set the slow cooker on "Low" and cook, covered for 6 hours.
3. Uncover the slow cooker and transfer 60 millilitres of the cooking liquid into a small bowl.
4. In the bowl with cooking liquid, add 15-20 grams of chickpeas and with a fork, mash until smooth.
5. In the slow cooker, add the mashed chickpeas, kale, lemon juice and remaining chickpeas and stir to combine.
6. Set the slow cooker on "Low" and cook, covered for 30 minutes.
7. Transfer the soup into serving bowls and drizzle each with oil.
8. Serve immediately.

Chickpeas & Veggie Stew

Servings|4   Time|8½ ours

Nutritional Content (per serving):

Cal| 353   Fat| 9.2g   Protein| 12.3g   Carbs| 56.4g

Ingredients:

- 30 millilitres olive oil
- 3 shallots, chopped
- 455 grams small red potatoes, quartered
- 255 grams frozen artichoke hearts
- 5 grams fresh thyme, minced
- 1 large bay leaf
- 90 millilitres dry white wine
- 360 millilitres vegetable broth
- 1 large carrot, peeled and sliced
- 2 garlic cloves, minced
- 1 red capsicum, seeded and chopped
- 1 (425-gram) can diced tomatoes
- 215 grams cooked chickpeas
- 5 grams fresh oregano, minced
- Salt and ground black pepper, as required

Directions:

1. In a skillet, heat the oil over medium heat and sauté the carrots, shallots and garlic for about 4-5 minutes.
2. Remove from the heat and transfer the carrot mixture into a slow cooker.
3. Add the remaining ingredients and stir to combine.
4. Set the slow cooker on "Low" and cook, covered for about 6-8 hours.
5. Serve hot.

Chicken & Carrot Stew

Servings|6   Time|6¼ hours

Nutritional Content (per serving):

Cal| 160   Fat| 4.8g   Protein| 19.1g   Carbs| 9.2g

Ingredients:

- 3 (115-gram) boneless chicken breast, cubed
- 2 celery stalks, chopped
- 2 garlic cloves, minced
- 2½ grams dried thyme
- 480 millilitres chicken broth
- 390 grams carrots, peeled and cubed
- 1 medium onion, sliced
- Salt and ground black pepper, as required

Directions:

1. In a slow cooker, add all ingredients and mix well.
2. Set the slow cooker on "Low" and cook, covered for 6 hours.
3. Serve hot.

Chicken & Black Beans Stew

Servings|4   Time|8½ ours

Nutritional Content (per serving):

Cal| 562   Fat| 13.5g   Protein| 54.4g   Carbs| 56.4g

Ingredients:

- 15 millilitres olive oil
- 2 garlic cloves, minced
- 200 grams tomatoes, chopped
- 170 grams canned white beans
- 2½ grams cayenne pepper
- 240 millilitres chicken broth
- 1 onion, chopped
- 455 grams chicken breasts
- 1 (425-gram) can black beans, rinsed and drained
- Salt and ground black pepper, as required

Directions:

1. In a large skillet, heat oil over medium heat and cook onions for about 5-6 minutes.
2. Add garlic and cook for about 1 minute.
3. Add chicken and cook for about 3-4 minutes per side or until browned.
4. Transfer the mixture into a slow cooker.
5. Add remaining ingredients and stir to combine.
6. Set the slow cooker on "Low" and cook, covered for 8 hours.
7. Uncover the slow cooker and transfer the chicken into a bowl.
8. With 2 forks, shred the breast meat completely.
9. Add shredded chicken into the beans mixture and serve hot.

Chicken & Quinoa Stew

Servings|8   Time|8 hours 20 minutes

Nutritional Content (per serving):

Cal| 278   Fat| 7g   Protein| 22.4g   Carbs| 33.1g

Ingredients:

- ❖ 15 millilitres olive oil
- ❖ 5 grams fresh ginger, minced
- ❖ 4 (115-gram) skinless, boneless chicken breasts
- ❖ 350 grams tomatoes, chopped
- ❖ 5 grams dried oregano, crushed
- ❖ Salt and ground black pepper, as required

- ❖ 1 medium onion, chopped
- ❖ 2 garlic cloves, minced
- ❖ 840 grams butternut squash, peeled and cubed
- ❖ 190 grams quinoa, rinsed
- ❖ 10 grams cayenne pepper
- ❖ 1680 millilitres vegetable broth

Directions:

1. In a skillet, heat oil over medium heat and sauté onion and garlic for about 4-5 minutes.
2. Transfer the onion mixture into a slow cooker.
3. Add remaining ingredients and stir to combine.
4. Set the slow cooker on "Low" and cook, covered for
5. Cover and cook for about 7-8 hours.
6. Uncover the slow cooker and transfer the chicken breasts into a bowl.
7. With 2 forks, shred the breast meat completely.
8. Add shredded chicken into squash mixture and serve hot.

Beef & Tomato Stew

Servings|8   Time|10¼ hours

Nutritional Content (per serving):

Cal| 371   Fat| 33.1g   Protein| 14.2g   Carbs| 3.6g

Ingredients:

- 680 grams lean boneless beef, cubed
- 480 millilitres beef broth
- 10 grams ground cumin
- 10 grams yellow curry paste
- 5 grams dried thyme, crushed
- 2 garlic cloves, minced
- 300 grams tomatoes, chopped
- 480 millilitres unsweetened almond milk
- Salt and ground black pepper, as required

Directions:

1. In a slow cooker, add all ingredients and mix well.
2. Set the slow cooker on "Low" and cook, covered for 8-10 hours.
3. Serve hot.

Beef & Cabbage Stew

Servings|8   Time|1 hours

Nutritional Content (per serving):

Cal| 259   Fat| 7.5g   Protein| 37.1g   Carbs| 9.8g

Ingredients:

- ❖ 1 medium head cabbage, chopped roughly
- ❖ 910 grams beef stew meat, cubed
- ❖ 400 grams tomatoes, chopped finely
- ❖ 10 grams fresh parsley, chopped
- ❖ 1 large onion, chopped
- ❖ 6 garlic cloves, minced
- ❖ Salt and ground black pepper, as required
- ❖ 240 millilitres beef broth

Directions:

1. Sprinkle the beef s with salt and black pepper generously.
2. In a slow cooker, place cabbage, onion and garlic and top with beef, followed by tomatoes.
3. Pour broth on top evenly.
4. Set the slow cooker on "Low" and cook, covered for 9 hours.
5. Serve with the garnishing of fresh parsley leaves.

Beef & Sweet Potato Stew

Servings|6   Time|7 hours 55 minutes

Nutritional Content (per serving):

Cal| 449   Fat| 15.8g   Protein| 51.7g   Carbs| 23.3g

Ingredients:

- ❖ 30 millilitres olive oil
- ❖ 2 onions, chopped
- ❖ 4 garlic cloves, minced
- ❖ 5 grams dried thyme, crushed
- ❖ Salt and ground black pepper, as required
- ❖ 2 large carrots, chopped
- ❖ 90 grams fresh spinach, torn
- ❖ 910 grams lean beef stew meat, cubed
- ❖ 5 grams fresh ginger, minced
- ❖ 15 grams curry powder
- ❖ 960 millilitres beef broth
- ❖ 45 millilitres fresh lemon juice
- ❖ 2 medium sweet potatoes, peeled and cubed

Directions:

1. In a large skillet, heat oil over medium heat and cook beef for about 4-5 minutes.
2. Transfer the beef into a bowl.
3. In the same skillet, add onion and sauté for about 3-4 minutes.
4. Add garlic, ginger, thyme and curry powder and sauté for 1 minute more.
5. Now transfer the cooked beef, onion mixture and remaining ingredients into a slow cooker.
6. Add remaining ingredients except for lemon juice and coriander and stir to combine.
7. Set the slow cooker on "Low" and cook, covered for 6-7½ hours.
8. Uncover the slow cooker and stir in spinach.
9. Set the slow cooker on "Low" and cook, covered for 30 minutes.

Pork & Onions Stew

Servings|6   Time|10¼ hours

Nutritional Content (per serving):

Cal| 354   Fat| 9.8g   Protein| 44.8g   Carbs| 13.8g

Ingredients:

- 910 grams boneless pork loin, cut into 1-inch pieces
- 2½ grams ground cinnamon
- 180 millilitres dry red wine
- 15 millilitres balsamic vinegar
- 190 grams frozen pearl onions
- 50 grams all-purpose flour
- 2½ grams dried thyme
- 1 (425-millilitre) can chicken broth
- 20 grams honey
- 115 grams feta cheese, crumbled

Directions:

1. In a bowl, add the pork cubes, flour, thyme and cinnamon and toss to coat well.
2. In another bowl, add broth, wine, vinegar and honey and beat until well combined.
3. In the bottom of a slow cooker, place the pork cubes and onions and top with broth mixture.
4. Set the slow cooker on "Low" and cook, covered for 9-10 hours.
5. Serve hot with the topping of feta cheese.

Pork & Cabbage Stew

Servings|8   Time|10¼ hours

Nutritional Content (per serving):

Cal| 404   Fat| 16.7g   Protein| 50.7g   Carbs| 10.7g

Ingredients:

- 2 small onions, sliced
- 225 grams baby carrots
- 1365 grams pork shoulder, cubed
- 2½ grams ground nutmeg
- 1 small head cabbage, chopped
- 20 grams fresh parsley, chopped
- 5 garlic cloves, minced
- Salt and ground black pepper, as required
- 5 grams ground cinnamon
- 15 millilitres fish sauce
- 15 millilitres apple cider vinegar

Directions:

1. In a slow cooker, add onions, garlic and baby carrots, season with salt and black pepper and toss well.
2. In a large bowl, place the pork cubes, cinnamon, nutmeg and fish sauce and mix well
3. Transfer the meat into the slow cooker.
4. Add in cabbage and vinegar and top with parsley.
5. Set the slow cooker on "Low" and cook, covered for 8-10 hours.
6. Serve hot.

Pork & Rutabaga Stew

Servings|10   Time|8¼ hours

Nutritional Content (per serving):

Cal| 278   Fat| 9g   Protein| 40.8g   Carbs| 6.9g

Ingredients:

- 1135 grams boneless country-style pork ribs
- 600 grams tomatoes, chopped finely
- 30 grams butter
- Salt and ground black pepper, as required
- 210 grams rutabaga, peeled and cubed
- 60 grams onion, chopped
- 2 garlic cloves, minced
- 960 millilitres chicken broth
- 5 grams oregano, minced

Directions:

1. In a slow cooker, add all ingredients and stir to combine.
2. Set the slow cooker on "Low" and cook, covered for 7½ hours.
3. Uncover the slow cooker and transfer pork onto a large plate.
4. With 2 forks, shred the pork completely.
5. Return the shredded pork into the slow cooker and stir well.
6. Set the slow cooker on "Low" and cook, covered for 30 minutes more.
7. Serve hot.

Pork & Plum Stew

Servings|6   Time|6¼ hours

Nutritional Content (per serving):

Cal| 359   Fat| 13.8g   Protein| 48.5g   Carbs| 7.3g

Ingredients:

- ❖ 910 grams pork tenderloin, cut into 2-inch pieces
- ❖ 2 celery stalks, chopped roughly
- ❖ 70 grams olives, pitted
- ❖ 4 garlic cloves, minced
- ❖ 2 bay leaves
- ❖ 1 fresh rosemary sprig
- ❖ 40 grams tomato paste
- ❖ 720 millilitres beef broth
- ❖ 2 large carrots, peeled and cut into ½-inch slices
- ❖ 1 medium onion, chopped
- ❖ 65 grams dried plums, pitted and chopped
- ❖ 1 fresh thyme sprig
- ❖ Salt and ground black pepper, as required

Directions:

1. In a slow cooker, place all the ingredients and stir to combine.
2. Set the slow cooker on "Low" and cook, covered for 5-6 hours.
3. Uncover the slow cooker and discard the bay leaves and herb sprigs.
4. Serve hot.

Lamb & Carrot Stew

Servings|6   Time|9¼ hours

Nutritional Content (per serving):

Cal| 284   Fat| 9.6g   Protein| 38.1g   Carbs| 8.6g

Ingredients:

- ❖ 780 grams lamb chops, trimmed
- ❖ 240 millilitres vegetable broth
- ❖ Salt and ground black pepper, as required
- ❖ 5 carrots, peeled and sliced thinly
- ❖ 2 onions, sliced thinly

Directions:

1. In a slow cooker, add all ingredients and mix well.
2. Set the slow cooker on "Low" and cook, covered for 7-9 hours.
3. Serve hot.

Lamb & Kale Stew

Servings|10   Time|6 hours 25 minutes

Nutritional Content (per serving):

Cal| 328   Fat| 16.1g   Protein| 39.9g   Carbs| 4.1g

Ingredients:

- 60 millilitres olive oil, divided
- 5 grams garlic powder
- Salt and ground black pepper, as required
- 5 grams dried oregano, crushed
- 75 grams carrot, peeled and chopped
- 480 millilitres chicken broth
- 1135 grams lean stewed lamb, cubed
- 2 small onions, chopped
- 5 grams dried thyme, crushed
- 5 grams dried basil, crushed
- 1 celery stalk, chopped
- 1 large tomato, chopped finely
- 45 millilitres fresh lemon juice

Directions:

1. In a large skillet, heat 30 millilitres of oil over medium-high heat and cook the lamb with garlic powder, salt and black pepper for about 4-5 minutes.
2. Transfer the lamb into a slow cooker.
3. In the same skillet, heat remaining oil over medium heat and sauté onions for about 4-5 minutes.
4. Transfer the onion mixture into the slow cooker.
5. Add remaining ingredients except for lemon juice and stir to combine.
6. Set the slow cooker on "Low" and cook, covered for 6 hours.
7. Uncover the slow cooker and with a slotted spoon, skim off the fats from top.
8. Serve this stew with the drizzling of fresh lemon juice.

Lamb & Chickpeas Stew

Servings|8   Time|6¼ hours

Nutritional Content (per serving):

Cal| 282   Fat| 9.6g   Protein| 29.5g   Carbs| 20.1g

Ingredients:

- 15 millilitres olive oil
- 1 (800-gram) diced tomatoes
- 1 large onion, chopped
- 10 grams ground coriander
- 1½ grams cayenne pepper
- 340 millilitres chicken broth
- 1 (425-gram) can chickpeas rinsed and drained
- 680 grams boneless lamb stew meat, cubed
- 4 garlic cloves, minced
- 10 grams ground cumin
- Salt and ground black pepper, as required
- 170 grams fresh spinach, torn

Directions:

1. In a large pan, heat oil over medium-high heat and cook the lamb for about 4-5 minutes.
2. In a slow cooker, add cooked lamb and remaining ingredients except for chickpeas and spinach and stir to combine.
3. Set the slow cooker on "Low" and cook, covered for 5½-6 hours.
4. Meanwhile, in a bowl, add 120 grams of chickpeas and with a fork, mash them.
5. Uncover the slow cooker and with a slotted spoon, skim off the fats from top.
6. Transfer the mashed chickpeas, remaining chickpeas and spinach in the slow cooker.
7. Now set the slow cooker on "High" and cook, covered for 5 minutes.
8. Serve hot.

Salmon & Veggie Stew

Servings|4   Time|6¼ hours

Nutritional Content (per serving):

Cal| 227   Fat| 13g   Protein| 24.7g   Carbs| 8.4g

Ingredients:

- ❖ 455 grams salmon fillet, cubed
- ❖ 1 medium onion, chopped
- ❖ 1 courgette, sliced
- ❖ 150 grams tomatoes, chopped
- ❖ 120 millilitres fish broth
- ❖ Salt and ground black pepper, as required

- ❖ 15 grams coconut oil
- ❖ 1 clove garlic, minced
- ❖ 1 green capsicum, seeded and cubed
- ❖ 1¼ grams dried oregano
- ❖ 1¼ grams dried basil

Directions:

1. In a slow cooker, add all ingredients and mix.
2. Set the slow cooker on "High" and cook, covered for 4-6 hours.
3. Serve hot.

Cod & Fennel Stew

Servings|8   Time|3 hours 55 minutes

Nutritional Content (per serving):

Cal| 181   Fat| 3g   Protein| 325.4g   Carbs| 14.3g

Ingredients:

- 2 large leeks, cut into ¼-inch-thick slices
- 2 garlic cloves, chopped
- 4 fresh thyme sprigs
- 60-120 millilitres dry white wine
- 1025 grams skinless cod fillets
- 625 grams fennel bulb, chopped
- 1025 grams tomatoes, chopped
- 8 fresh parsley sprigs
- Salt and ground black pepper, as required
- 10 millilitres olive oil

Directions:

1. In a slow cooker, place all the ingredients except for cod and oil and stir to combine.
2. Set the slow cooker on "High" and cook, covered for 3 hours.
3. Uncover the slow cooker and place fish on top of the stew.
4. Set the slow cooker on "High" and cook, covered for 30-40 minutes.
5. Uncover the slow cooker and discard the herb sprigs.
6. Divide the stew into serving bowls.
7. Drizzle with oil and serve.

Curried Seafood Stew

Servings|8   Time|5 hours 10 minutes

Nutritional Content (per serving):

Cal| 279   Fat| 8.1g   Protein| 36.4g   Carbs| 14.9g

Ingredients:

- 30 millilitres olive oil
- 2 large fennel bulbs, trimmed and chopped finely
- 6 sprigs fresh parsley
- 240 millilitres chicken broth
- 780 grams shrimp, peeled and deveined
- 910 grams tomatoes, chopped
- 2 garlic cloves, minced
- 10 grams curry powder
- Salt and ground black pepper, as required
- 780 grams mussels, removed beards and scrubbed

Directions:

1. In a slow cooker, add all ingredients except for seafood and stir to combine.
2. Set the slow cooker on "High" and cook, covered for 3-4 hours.
3. Uncover the slow cooker and stir in seafood.
4. Set the slow cooker on "High" and cook, covered for 50 minutes more.
5. Serve hot.

Seafood & Potato Stew

Servings|6   Time|4 hours 20 minutes

Nutritional Content (per serving):

Cal| 285   Fat| 3.4g   Protein| 35.7g   Carbs| 21.8g

Ingredients:

- 1 (680-gram) can crushed tomatoes
- 3 garlic cloves, minced
- ½ of medium onion, chopped
- 5 grams dried coriander
- 5 grams dried basil
- 1¼ grams red pepper flakes
- 455 grams extra-large shrimp, peeled and deveined
- 225 grams crab legs
- 960 millilitres vegetable broth
- 120 millilitres white wine
- 455 grams baby potatoes, cut into bite-sized pieces
- 5 grams dried thyme
- 1½ grams celery salt
- Salt and ground black pepper, as required
- 225 grams scallops

Directions:

1. In a slow cooker, place all the ingredients except for seafood and stir to combine.
2. Set the slow cooker on "High" and cook, covered for 2-3 hours.
3. Uncover the slow cooker and stir in the seafood.
4. Set the slow cooker on "High" and cook, covered for 30-60 minutes.
5. Serve hot.

Casserole Recipes

Cauliflower Casserole

Servings|6   Time|4¼ hours

Nutritional Content (per serving):

Cal| 187   Fat| 13.8g   Protein| 9.9g   Carbs| 7g

Ingredients:

- ❖ 680 grams frozen cauliflower
- ❖ 115 grams mozzarella cheese, shredded
- ❖ 3 green onions, chopped
- ❖ 115 grams cream cheese, cubed
- ❖ 115 grams cheddar cheese, shredded

Directions:

1. Grease a slow cooker.
2. In the prepared slow cooker, place half of the cauliflower in an even layer.
3. Place half of cream cheese cubes over cauliflower, followed by half of both cheeses.
4. Repeat the layers once.
5. Set the slow cooker on "Low" and cook, covered for 4 hours.
6. Serve hot with the garnishing of stallion.

Chickpeas, Macaroni & Veggie Casserole

Servings|5   Time|8¼ hours

Nutritional Content (per serving):

Cal| 506   Fat| 8.4g   Protein| 25.7g   Carbs| 87.1g

Ingredients:

- 1 (425-gram) can chickpeas, rinsed and drained
- 1 medium onion, chopped
- 2 garlic cloves, chopped finely
- 1 (150-gram) can Italian-style tomato paste
- 5 grams Italian seasoning
- 22g grams frozen cut green beans, thawed
- 55 grams Parmesan cheese, shredded
- 3 medium carrots, peeled and sliced
- 1 (790-gram) can diced tomatoes with juice
- 240 millilitres water
- 10 grams sugar
- Salt and ground black pepper, as required
- 150 grams uncooked elbow macaroni

Directions:

1. In a slow cooker, place all the ingredients except for green beans, macaroni and parmesan cheese and stir to combine.
2. Set the slow cooker on "Low" and cook, covered for about 6-8 hours.
3. Uncover the slow cooker and stir in the green beans and macaroni.
4. Set the slow cooker on "High" and cook, covered for about 20 minutes.
5. Top with cheese and serve hot.

Beans & Veggie Casserole

Servings|6   Time|6¼ hours

Nutritional Content (per serving):

Cal| 186   Fat| 3.7g   Protein| 10.5g   Carbs| 29.7g

Ingredients:

- 2 (425-gram) cans cannellini beans, rinsed and drained
- 150 grams courgette, chopped
- 90 grams Kalamata olives, pitted and halved
- 2 garlic cloves, minced
- 30 millilitres balsamic vinegar
- 30 millilitres fresh lemon juice
- 30 grams feta cheese, crumbled
- 1 (400-gram) can diced tomatoes with basil, garlic and oregano
- 150 grams red capsicum, seeded and chopped
- 20 grams parsley, chopped
- Salt and ground black pepper, as required
- 240 millilitres vegetable broth

Directions:

1. In a slow cooker, place all the ingredients except for cheese and stir to combine.
2. Set the slow cooker on "Low" and cook, covered for 4 hours.
3. Serve hot with the topping of feta cheese.

Chicken & Ham Casserole

Servings|8   Time|15¼ hours

Nutritional Content (per serving):

Cal| 421   Fat| 20.4g   Protein| 51.3g   Carbs| 9.1g

Ingredients:

- 1365 grams chicken tenderloins
- 455 grams fresh Cremini mushrooms, sliced
- 225 grams cream cheese, softened
- 300 grams cream of mushroom soup with roasted garlic
- 230 grams mozzarella cheese, shredded
- Salt and ground black pepper, as required
- 20 grams fresh basil, chopped
- 300 grams cream of chicken soup with herbs
- 120 millilitres chicken broth
- 455 grams ham slices
- 20 grams parsley, chopped

Directions:

1. Season the chicken tenderloins with salt and black pepper generously.
2. In the bottom of a slow cooker, place the chicken tenderloins, followed by the mushrooms and basil.
3. In a bowl, add the cream cheese, cream soups and broth and with an electric mixer, mix for about 2-4 minutes cream cheese mixture on top of mushrooms.
4. Arrange the ham slices on top and sprinkle with the mozzarella cheese.
5. Set the slow cooker on "Low" and cook, covered for 4-5 hours.
6. Serve with the garnishing of parsley.

Chicken, Artichoke & Olives Casserole

Servings|6   Time|7 hours 19 minutes

Nutritional Content (per serving):

Cal| 410   Fat| 14.2g   Protein| 53.1g   Carbs| 0.9g

Ingredients:

- ❖ 15 millilitres vegetable oil
- ❖ 1 (395-gram) can artichoke hearts
- ❖ 1 (960-millilitre) container beef broth
- ❖ 90 grams Kalamata olives, pitted
- ❖ 5 grams dried oregano
- ❖ 5 grams dried parsley
- ❖ 2½ grams ground cumin
- ❖ 910 grams beef stew meat
- ❖ 1 onion, chopped
- ❖ 4 garlic cloves, chopped
- ❖ 1 (425-gram) can tomato sauce
- ❖ 1 (425-gram) can diced tomatoes with juice
- ❖ 5 grams dried basil
- ❖ 1 bay leaf, crumbled

Directions:

1. In a skillet, heat the oil over medium-high heat and cook the beef for about 2 minutes per side.
2. Transfer the beef into a slow cooker and top with artichoke hearts, followed by the onion and garlic.
3. Place the remaining ingredients on top.
4. Set the slow cooker on "Low" and cook, covered for 7 hours.
5. Serve hot.

Chicken & Potato Casserole

Servings|8   Time|8 hours 21 minutes

Nutritional Content (per serving):

Cal| 497   Fat| 21.6g   Protein| 55.5g   Carbs| 18.7g

Ingredients:

- 2½ grams dried oregano
- 1¼ grams dried rosemary
- 8 bone-in, skin-on chicken thighs
- 30 grams butter
- 30 millilitres olive oil
- 4 garlic cloves, minced
- 110 grams Parmesan cheese, grated
- 2½ grams dried basil
- Salt and ground black pepper, as required
- 910 grams baby red potatoes, quartered
- 2½ grams dried thyme
- 10 grams parsley, chopped

Directions:

1. In a bowl, add the oregano, basil, rosemary, salt and black pepper and mix well.
2. Season the chicken thighs with herb mixture generously.
3. In a large skillet, melt the butter over medium-high heat.
4. Place the chicken thighs, skin-side down and cook for about 2-3 minutes.
5. Flip and cook for about 2-3 minutes.
6. In a greased slow cooker, place the potatoes and stir in the oil, garlic and thyme, salt and black pepper.
7. Arrange the chicken thighs on top in an even layer.
8. Set the slow cooker on "Low" and cook, covered for 7-8 hours.
9. Top with Parmesan and parsley and serve immediately.

Chicken & Orzo Casserole

Servings|4   Time|3¼ hours

Nutritional Content (per serving):

Cal| 652   Fat| 3.3g   Protein| 58.3g   Carbs| 28.4g

Ingredients:

- 4 boneless, skinless chicken breasts
- Salt and ground black pepper, as required
- 1 medium onion, chopped finely
- 55 grams butter, melted
- 150 grams orzo pasta
- 55 grams Parmesan cheese, shredded

- 15 grams Italian seasoning, divided
- 15 millilitres olive oil
- 100 grams fresh mushrooms, sliced
- 720 millilitres low-sodium chicken broth

Directions:

1. Season the chicken breasts with little Italian seasonings, salt and black pepper evenly.
2. In a large non-stick skillet, heat the oil over medium-high heat and cook the chicken breasts for about 5 minutes, flipping once halfway through.
3. Transfer the chicken breasts into a greased slow cooker.
4. Top with mushrooms, onions, garlic, butter, broth, salt and black pepper.
5. Set the slow cooker on "High" and cook, covered for 1-2 hours.
6. Remove the lid and stir in the orzo.
7. Set the slow cooker on "High" and cook, covered for 30-45 minutes.
8. Remove the lid and with a slotted spoon, transfer the chicken into a bowl.
9. With 2 forks, shred the chicken meat.
10. Return the shredded chicken into the slow cooker and stir to combine.
11. Sprinkle the top with the Parmesan cheese evenly.
12. Set the slow cooker on "High" and cook, covered for 5-10 minutes.
13. Serve hot.

Beef & Mushroom Casserole

Servings|8   Time|8¼ hours

Nutritional Content (per serving):

Cal| 292   Fat| 7.9g   Protein| 40g   Carbs| 16.1g

Ingredients:

- ❖ 910 grams beef stew meat, cubed
- ❖ 4 garlic cloves, minced
- ❖ 40 grams fresh parsley, chopped
- ❖ Salt and ground black pepper, as required
- ❖ 200 grams fresh mushrooms, sliced
- ❖ 600 grams tomato paste
- ❖ 480 millilitres beef broth

Directions:

1. In a slow cooker, add all ingredients except lemon juice and stir to combine.
2. Set the slow cooker on "Low" and cook, covered for 8 hours.
3. Serve hot with the drizzling of lemon juice

Beef & Green Beans Casserole

Servings|4   Time|4½ hours

Nutritional Content (per serving):

Cal| 353   Fat| 7.3g   Protein| 442.2g   Carbs| 30.4g

Ingredients:

- ❖ 455 grams beef stew meat, cubed
- ❖ 1 medium onion, chopped
- ❖ 1 (910-gram) can crushed tomatoes
- ❖ 20 grams parsley, chopped
- ❖ 455 grams fresh green beans, trimmed and cut in 2-inch pieces
- ❖ 10 grams ground cinnamon
- ❖ Salt and ground black pepper, as required

Directions:

1. In a slow cooker, place all the ingredients except for the parsley and stir to combine.
2. Set the slow cooker on "High" and cook, covered for 4 hours.
3. Serve hot with the garnishing of parsley.

Ground Beef & Pasta Casserole

Servings|6   Time|9 hours

Nutritional Content (per serving):

Cal| 323   Fat| 7.3g   Protein| 32g   Carbs| 32.1g

Ingredients:

- ❖ 455 grams ground beef
- ❖ 1 onion, chopped
- ❖ 150 grams tomato paste
- ❖ Salt and ground black pepper, as required
- ❖ 240 millilitres water
- ❖ 4 garlic cloves, minced
- ❖ 300 grams tomatoes, chopped
- ❖ 5 grams parsley, minced
- ❖ 720 millilitres beef broth
- ❖ 200 grams uncooked whole-wheat shell pasta

Directions:

1. In a slow cooker, add all ingredients except for the pasta and stir to combine.
2. Set the slow cooker on "Low" and cook, covered for 7-8 hours.
3. Uncover the slow cooker and stir in pasta and water.
4. Now, set the slow cooker on "High" and cook, covered for 40-45 minutes.
5. Serve hot.

Pork & Veggie Casserole

Servings|4   Time|8¼ hours

Nutritional Content (per serving):

Cal| 269   Fat| 8.1g   Protein| 38.6g   Carbs| 9.8g

Ingredients:

- 455 grams boneless pork meat, cut into thin strips
- 1 medium onion, sliced
- 100 grams fresh mushrooms, sliced
- Salt and ground black pepper, as required
- 300 grams tomatoes, chopped
- 190 grams fresh green beans
- 120 millilitres beef broth

Directions:

1. In a slow cooker, add all ingredients and stir to combine.
2. Set the slow cooker on "Low" and cook, covered for 8 hours.
3. Serve hot.

Ham & Veggie Casserole

Servings|6   Time|1¾ hours

Nutritional Content (per serving):

Cal| 233   Fat| 16.2g   Protein| 17.2g   Carbs| 4.5g

Ingredients:

- ❖ 6 large eggs
- ❖ 65 millilitres unsweetened coconut milk
- ❖ 2½ grams garlic powder
- ❖ 150 grams ham, chopped
- ❖ 115 grams pepper jack cheese, shredded
- ❖ 125 grams plain Greek yogurt
- ❖ 1½ grams dried thyme, crushed
- ❖ Salt and ground black pepper, as required
- ❖ 55 grams fresh spinach, chopped
- ❖ 40 grams fresh mushrooms, sliced

Directions:

1. Grease a slow cooker.
2. In a bowl, add eggs, yogurt, milk, thyme, garlic powder, salt and black pepper and beat until smooth.
3. Stir in ham, kale, mushrooms and cheese.
4. Place egg mixture into prepared slow cooker.
5. Set the slow cooker on "High" and cook, covered for 1½ hours.
6. Serve hot.

Sausage & Broccoli Casserole

Servings|6   Time|5¼ hours

Nutritional Content (per serving):

Cal| 495   Fat| 41g   Protein| 26.9g   Carbs| 5g

Ingredients:

- ❖ 10 eggs
- ❖ 2 garlic cloves, minced
- ❖ Salt and ground black pepper, as required
- ❖ 1 (340-gram) package turkey sausage, cooked and sliced
- ❖ 180 grams heavy cream
- ❖ 2½ grams red pepper flakes, crushed
- ❖ 1 medium head broccoli, chopped
- ❖ 115 grams cheddar cheese, shredded

Directions:

1. In a bowl, add eggs, cream, red pepper flakes, salt and black pepper and beat until well combined.
2. Grease a slow cooker.
3. In the bottom of the prepared slow cooker, place ½ of the broccoli, followed by ½ of the sausage and ½ of the cheese. Repeat the layers once.
4. Place the egg mixture on top evenly.
5. Set the slow cooker on "Low" and cook, covered for 4-5 hours.
6. Serve hot.

Bacon & Veggie Casserole

Servings|8   Time|8 hours 20 minutes

Nutritional Content (per serving):

Cal| 523   Fat| 3.3g   Protein| 30.8g   Carbs| 15.6g

Ingredients:

- 15 grams coconut oil
- 1 green capsicum, seeded and chopped
- Pinch of red pepper flakes, crushed
- 250 millilitres unsweetened coconut milk
- 455 grams cooked bacon, chopped
- 1 onion, chopped
- 2 garlic cloves, minced
- 2 large sweet potatoes, peeled and grated
- 12 eggs
- 5 grams dried dill, crushed
- Salt and ground black pepper, as required

Directions:

1. In a large skillet, heat oil over medium heat and sauté onion, capsicum and garlic for about 4-5 minutes.
2. Remove from the heat and set aside.
3. Meanwhile, in a bowl, add sweet potato and red pepper flakes and toss to coat well.
4. In another bowl, add eggs, coconut milk, salt and black pepper and beat until well combined.
5. Grease a large slow cooker.
6. In the bottom of the prepared slow cooker, place 1/3 of the grated sweet potatoes, followed by 1/3 of the onion mixture and 1/3 of the bacon.
7. Repeat the layers twice. Place the egg mixture on top evenly.
8. Set the slow cooker on "Low" and cook, covered for 6-8 hours.
9. Cut into equal-sized wedges and serve.

Lamb & Apricot Casserole

Servings|6   Time|8 hours 10 minutes

Nutritional Content (per serving):

Cal| 203   Fat| 7.8g   Protein| 23.2g   Carbs| 10.9g

Ingredients:

- ❖ 10 grams coconut oil
- ❖ 5 grams ground coriander
- ❖ 455 grams boneless lamb meat, cubed
- ❖ 2 cloves garlic, minced
- ❖ 5 grams ground cumin
- ❖ 5 grams ground cinnamon
- ❖ 1 150 grams tomato paste
- ❖ 1 onion, chopped
- ❖ 165 grams dried apricots

Directions:

1. In a bowl, add oil, cumin, coriander and cinnamon and mix until well combined.
2. Add lamb cubes and coat with mixture generously.
3. Heat a non-stick skillet over medium heat and cook the lamb cubes for about 4-5 minutes or until browned.
4. Transfer the cooked lamb into a slow cooker.
5. Add remaining ingredients and stir to combine.
6. Set the slow cooker on "Low" and cook, covered for 6-8 hours.
7. Serve hot.

Salmon & Sweet Potato Casserole

Servings|5   Time|10¼ hours

Nutritional Content (per serving):

Cal| 236   Fat| 6.4g   Protein| 20.7g   Carbs| 24.4g

Ingredients:

- ❖ 3 sweet potatoes, peeled and sliced thinly
- ❖ 455 grams salmon fillets, cubed
- ❖ 360 millilitres fish broth

- ❖ Salt and ground black pepper, as required
- ❖ 1 medium onion, chopped
- ❖ Pinch of ground nutmeg

Directions:

1. In a slow cooker, place half of the sweet potatoes and sprinkle with salt and black pepper.
2. Place half salmon cubes o top, followed by half of onion.
3. Repeat the layers and top with broth.
4. Sprinkle nutmeg on top.
5. Set the slow cooker on "Low" and cook, covered for 8-10 hours.
6. Serve hot.

Haddock & Olives Casserole

Servings|4   Time|2 hours 35 minutes

Nutritional Content (per serving):

Cal| 177   Fat| 2.8g   Protein| 29.7g   Carbs| 7.7g

Ingredients:

- 455 grams haddock fillets, cubed
- 3 garlic cloves, minced
- 1¼ grams cayenne pepper
- 120 millilitres chicken broth
- 2 large tomatoes, chopped
- 10 grams fresh coriander leaves, chopped
- 1 small onion, thinly sliced
- 5 grams dried dill weed, crushed
- Salt and ground black pepper, as required
- 45 grams black olives, potted

Directions:

1. In the bottom of a slow cooker, place haddock fillets.
2. Place onion and garlic over haddock.
3. Sprinkle with dill, cayenne pepper, salt and black pepper.
4. Pour broth on top.
5. Set the slow cooker on "Low" and cook, covered for 1½ hours.
6. Uncover the slow cooker and stir in tomatoes and olives.
7. Set the slow cooker on "Low" and cook, covered for 30-50 minutes more.
8. Garnish with coriander and serve.

Salmon & Capsicum Casserole

Servings|4   Time|6 hours

Nutritional Content (per serving):

Cal| 225   Fat| 11.1g   Protein| 24.1g   Carbs| 9g

Ingredients:

- 455 grams skinless salmon fillet, cubed
- 2 red capsicum, seeded and cubed
- 1¼ grams dried rosemary, crushed
- 15 millilitres olive oil
- 1 medium onion, chopped
- 1 clove garlic, minced
- 150 grams tomatoes, chopped
- 120 millilitres fish broth
- 1¼ grams dried basil, crushed
- Salt and ground black pepper, as required

Directions:

1. In a slow cooker, add all ingredients and mix.
2. Set the slow cooker on "High" and cook, covered for 4-6 hours
3. Serve hot.

Shrimp & Tomato Casserole

Servings|6   Time|6 hours

Nutritional Content (per serving):

Cal| 242   Fat| 12.8g   Protein| 20g   Carbs| 13.1g

Ingredients:

- 250 millilitres unsweetened coconut milk
- 50 grams celery, chopped
- 800 grams tomatoes, chopped
- 10 grams fresh basil, chopped
- 455 grams shrimp, shelled and deveined
- 20 grams fresh parsley, chopped

- 1 onion, chopped
- 1 yellow capsicum, seeded and sliced thinly
- 30 grams red curry paste
- Salt and ground black pepper, as required

Directions:

1. In a slow cooker, add all ingredients except shrimp and mix well.
2. Set the slow cooker on "Low" and cook, covered for 5 hours 20 minutes.
3. Uncover the slow cooker and stir in shrimp.
4. Set the slow cooker on "Low" and cook, covered for 40 minutes.
5. Top with parsley and serve.

Shrimp & Capsicum Casserole

Servings|8   Time|3¾ hours

Nutritional Content (per serving):

Cal| 148   Fat| 1.9g   Protein| 21.3g   Carbs| 12.1g

Ingredients:

- ❖ 225 grams red capsicum, seeded and sliced
- ❖ 600 grams tomatoes, chopped finely
- ❖ 1½ grams dried thyme, crushed
- ❖ 1¼ grams cayenne pepper
- ❖ 1¼ grams red pepper flakes, crushed
- ❖ 680 grams shrimp, peeled and deveined
- ❖ 225 grams green capsicum, seeded and sliced
- ❖ 1 garlic clove, minced
- ❖ 300 grams tomato sauce
- ❖ 1½ grams dried basil, crushed
- ❖ 5 grams lemon pepper
- ❖ Salt and ground black pepper, as required

Directions:

1. In a slow cooker, mix together all ingredients except for shrimp.
2. Set the slow cooker on "High" and cook, covered for 2-3 hours.
3. Uncover and stir in shrimp.
4. Set the slow cooker on "High" and cook, covered for 30 minutes.
5. Serve hot.

Risotto & Pilaf Recipes

Simple Risotto

Servings|6   Time|3 hours

Nutritional Content (per serving):

Cal| 325   Fat| 13.1g   Protein| 8.9g   Carbs| 40g

Ingredients:

- ❖ 275 grams Arborio rice
- ❖ 60 millilitres olive oil
- ❖ 4 cloves garlic, minced
- ❖ Salt and ground black pepper, as required

- ❖ 740 millilitres hot chicken broth
- ❖ 60 millilitres white wine
- ❖ 5 grams dried onion flakes
- ❖ 75 grams Parmesan cheese, shredded

Directions:

1. In a slow cooker, add all ingredients except for Parmesan cheese and stir to combine.
2. Set the slow cooker on "High" and cook, covered for 2-2½ hours.
3. Uncover and stir in the Parmesan cheese.
4. Set the slow cooker on "High" and cook, uncovered for 15 minutes.
5. Serve hot.

Leek Risotto

Servings|6   Time|2 hours 18 minutes

Nutritional Content (per serving):

Cal| 497   Fat| 13.3g   Protein| 16.3g   Carbs| 69.8g

Ingredients:

- 55 grams butter, divided
- 2 garlic cloves, minced
- 240 millilitres white wine
- Salt and ground black pepper, as required
- 110 grams Parmesan cheese, grated
- 3 leeks, sliced thinly
- 440 grams Arborio rice
- 5 grams fresh thyme, minced
- 1320 millilitres hot chicken broth
- 15 millilitres fresh lemon juice
- 5 grams lemon peel, grated finely

Directions:

1. In a large non-stick skillet, melt 15 grams of butter over medium heat and sauté leeks and garlic for about 2-3 minutes.
2. Add rice and sauté for about 1-2 minutes.
3. Stir in wine and cook for about 3 minutes, stirring continuously or until all the liquid is absorbed.
4. Transfer the rice mixture into a greased slow cooker.
5. Add thyme, salt, black pepper and hot broth and mix well.
6. Set the slow cooker on "High" and cook, covered for 2 hours.
7. Uncover and immediately stir in remaining butter, cheese and lemon juice.
8. Serve immediately with the topping of lemon peel.

Asparagus Risotto

Servings|6   Time|2¼ hours

Nutritional Content (per serving):

Cal| 527   Fat| 21.4g   Protein| 14.1g   Carbs| 67g

Ingredients:

- 45 millilitres olive oil
- 3 garlic cloves, minced
- 90 millilitres white wine
- 10 grams lemon zest, grated
- Salt and ground black pepper, as required
- 45 grams Parmesan cheese, grated
- 120 grams onion, chopped
- 440 grams Arborio rice
- 1320 millilitres vegetable broth
- 30 millilitres fresh lemon juice
- 455 grams asparagus, trimmed and cut into 1-inch pieces
- 80 grams butter

Directions:

1. Heat the oil in a large skillet over medium-high heat and sauté the onion for about 4-6 minutes.
2. Add the garlic and sauté for about 1 minute.
3. Stir in the rice and cook for about 3 minutes, stirring continuously.
4. Add the wine and cook for about 3-5 minutes or until almost all the liquid is absorbed, stirring continuously.
5. Transfer the rice mixture into a slow cooker.
6. Pour in the broth and lemon juice and then sprinkle with lemon zest, salt, and black pepper.
7. Set the slow cooker on "High" and cook, covered for 1½ hours.
8. Uncover the slow cooker and stir in the asparagus.
9. Set the slow cooker on "High" and cook, covered for 30 minutes.
10. Remove the lid and stir in the butter and Parmesan cheese.
11. Serve immediately.

Mushroom Risotto

Servings|4   Time|3 hours 35 minutes

Nutritional Content (per serving):

Cal| 425   Fat| 5.3g   Protein| 18.8g   Carbs| 72.3g

Ingredients:

- 1 liter vegetable broth
- 5 millilitres olive oil
- 250 grams fresh chestnut mushrooms, sliced
- Salt and ground black pepper, as required
- 35 grams Parmesan cheese, grated
- 50 grams dried porcini mushrooms
- 1 onion, chopped finely
- 300 grams bsmati rice
- 15 grams fresh parsley, chopped finely

Directions:

1. In a saucepan, add the broth and porcini mushrooms and bring to a boil.
2. Remove from the heat and set aside for 10 minutes.
3. In a skillet, heat the oil over medium heat and cook the onion for about 8-10 minutes, stirring frequently.
4. Add the mushroom and cook for about 5-6 minutes, stirring frequently.
5. Transfer the mushroom mixture into a slow cooker.
6. Add the rice and stir to combine.
7. Through a fine sieve, strain the broth mixture into the slow cooker.
8. Set the slow cooker on "High" and cook, covered for 3 hours, stirring once halfway through.
9. Uncover the slow cooker and stir in the parsley, salt and black pepper.
10. Sprinkle with Parmesan and serve immediately.

Cauliflower & Peas Risotto

Servings|6   Time|1 hour 20 minutes

Nutritional Content (per serving):

Cal| 288   Fat| 9.6g   Protein| 9.5g   Carbs| 37.5g

Ingredients:

- 40 grams butter
- 90 millilitres dry white wine
- 220 grams Arborio rice
- 840 millilitres chicken broth, warmed
- 145 grams frozen peas, thawed
- 120 grams onion, chopped
- ½ of large head cauliflower, chopped
- 55 grams Cheddar cheese, grated and divided

Directions:

1. In a skillet, melt butter over medium heat and sauté the onion for about 5-6 minutes.
2. Add the rice and cook for about 3 minute.
3. Add the cauliflower and cook for about 3 minutes.
4. Add wine and cook for about 1½-2 minutes.
5. Transfer the rice mixture into a slow cooker and top with hot broth.
6. Set the slow cooker on "High" and cook, covered for 50 minutes.
7. Uncover the slow cooker and stir in the peas and 30 grams of cheese.
8. Set the slow cooker on "High" and cook, covered for 10-15 minutes.
9. Serve immediately with the garnishing of remaining cheese.

Chicken Risotto

Servings|6   Time|2 hours 25 minutes

Nutritional Content (per serving):

Cal| 491   Fat| 12.5g   Protein| 25.2g   Carbs| 63.3g

Ingredients:

- ❖ 15 millilitres olive oil
- ❖ 1 brown onion, chopped finely
- ❖ 440 grams Arborio rice
- ❖ 2 (150-gram) boneless chicken breasts, chopped
- ❖ 55 grams Parmesan cheese, grated
- ❖ 25g butter
- ❖ 2 cloves garlic, crushed
- ❖ 120 millilitres white wine
- ❖ 720 millilitres hot chicken broth
- ❖ 2 fresh rosemary sprigs

Directions:

1. In a large frypan, heat oil and butter. Over medium heat and sauté the onion and garlic for about 3-8 minutes.
2. Add the rice and stir to combine.
3. Pour in wine and cook for about 2-3 minutes.
4. Transfer the rice mixture into a slow cooker and top with chicken pieces, followed by hot broth.
5. Sprinkle with salt and pepper and top with rosemary sprigs.
6. Set the slow cooker on "High" and cook, covered for 2 hours, stirring once halfway through.
7. Uncover the slow cooker and stir in the Parmesan.
8. Serve immediately.

Chicken & Mushroom Risotto

Servings|4   Time|1½ hours

Nutritional Content (per serving):

Cal| 796   Fat| 24.6g   Protein| 37.3g   Carbs| 99.7g

Ingredients:

- ❖ 30 millilitres olive oil
- ❖ 200 grams button mushrooms, halved
- ❖ 1 brown onion, chopped finely
- ❖ 15 grams fresh thyme leaves, chopped and divided
- ❖ 480 millilitres water
- ❖ 250 grams cooked chicken, shredded
- ❖ 4 Portobello mushrooms, sliced thinly
- ❖ 50 grams butter
- ❖ 4 garlic cloves, crushed
- ❖ 120 millilitres dry white wine
- ❖ 960 millilitres chicken broth
- ❖ 440 grams Arborio rice
- ❖ 55 grams Parmesan cheese, grated finely

Directions:

1. In a skillet, heat the oil over medium heat and cook the mushrooms for about 6-7 minutes, stirring frequently.
2. Transfer the mushrooms into a bowl.
3. In the same skillet, melt butter over medium-high heat and sauté onion, garlic and half the thyme for about 5 minutes.
4. Add the wine, broth and water and bring to a boil.
5. In a slow cooker, place the rice and broth mixture and stir to combine.
6. Set the slow cooker on "High" and cook, covered for 45 minutes.
7. Uncover the slow cooker and stir in the chicken and mushrooms.
8. Set the slow cooker on "High" and cook, covered for 15 minutes.
9. Uncover the slow cooker and stir in the Parmesan, salt and black pepper.
10. Serve immediately with the garnishing of remaining thyme.

Bacon & Mushroom Risotto

Servings|4   Time|2 hours 10 minutes

Nutritional Content (per serving):

Cal| 747   Fat| 33.5g   Protein| 32.3g   Carbs| 74.8g

Ingredients:

- 6 bacon slices, chopped
- 60 grams shallots, chopped finely
- 330 grams uncooked Arborio rice
- 720 millilitres chicken broth
- 55 grams Parmesan cheese, grated
- 225 grams fresh mushrooms, sliced
- Salt, as required
- 60 millilitres dry white wine
- 120 grams warm heavy whipping cream

Directions:

1. Grease a slow cooker.
2. Heat 12-inch skillet over medium heat and cook the bacon for about 8-10 minutes, stirring frequently.
3. With a slotted spoon, transfer the bacon into the prepared slow cooker.
4. In the skillet, add the mushrooms over medium-high heat and cook for about 4-6 minutes, stirring occasionally.
5. Stir in the shallots and cook for about 2-4 minutes, stirring frequently.
6. Add the rice and salt and cook for about 2 minutes, stirring frequently.
7. Add wine and cook for about 2-3 minutes or until most of the liquid is absorbed.
8. Transfer the rice mixture into the slow cooker and top with broth.
9. Set the slow cooker on "High" and cook, covered for 1½ hours, stirring once after 30 minutes.
10. Uncover the slow cooker and stir in the warm cream and Parmesan.
11. Serve immediately.

Ham & Peas Risotto

Servings|6   Time|2 hours

Nutritional Content (per serving):

Cal| 518   Fat| 25.3g   Protein| 20.1g   Carbs| 70g

Ingredients:

- ❖ 60 grams butter, divided
- ❖ 1 shallot, minced
- ❖ 1080 millilitres hot chicken broth
- ❖ 220 grams frozen baby peas, thawed
- ❖ 110 grams Parmesan cheese, grated
- ❖ 1 onion, chopped finely
- ❖ 440 grams Arborio rice
- ❖ 120 millilitres white wine
- ❖ Salt and ground black pepper, as required
- ❖ 115 grams cooked ham, chopped

Directions:

1. In a medium saucepan, melt half of the butter over medium-low heat and sauté the onion and shallot for about 4-6 minutes.
2. Add the rice and cook for about 3-4 minutes, stirring frequently.
3. Transfer the rice mixture into a slow cooker and stir in broth and wine.
4. Set the slow cooker on "High" and cook, covered for 1¼ hours, stirring once after 1 hour of cooking.
5. Uncover the slow cooker and stir in the peas, ham and remaining butter.
6. Set the slow cooker on "High" and cook, covered for 20 minutes.
7. Uncover the slow cooker and stir in the Parmesan.
8. Serve immediately.

Sausage & Veggie Risotto

Servings|6   Time|1 hour 20 minutes

Nutritional Content (per serving):

Cal| 654   Fat| 30.2g   Protein| 25.6g   Carbs| 64.8g

Ingredients:

- 340 grams sweet Italian sausages, casings removed
- 120 millilitres dry white wine
- 1 medium courgette, cut into ½-inch pieces
- Salt, as required
- 85 grams Parmigiano-Reggiano cheese, grated

- 70 grams butter, divided
- 1 small onion, chopped
- 440 grams Arborio rice
- 1080 millilitres hot chicken broth
- 150 grams fresh baby spinach
- Ground black pepper, as required

Directions:

1. Heat a lightly greased skillet over medium-high heat and cook the sausage for about 10 minutes.
2. Transfer the cooked sausage into a slow cooker.
3. In the same skillet, melt 40 grams of butter over medium heat and sauté the onion for about 4 minutes.
4. Add the wine and cook for about 2 minutes, scraping up any browned bits from the bottom.
5. Stir in the rice and cook for about 2-3 minutes, stirring frequently.
6. Transfer the rice mixture into the slow cooker with courgette, hot broth and salt.
7. Set the slow cooker on "High" and cook, covered for 1 hour, stirring once halfway through.
8. Uncover the slow cooker and immediately stir in the spinach until just wilted.
9. Stir in the remaining butter, cheese and black pepper and serve immediately.

Rice & Cherries Pilaf

Servings|6   Time|3¼ hours

Nutritional Content (per serving):

Cal| 206   Fat| 2g   Protein| 6.4g   Carbs| 40g

Ingredients:

- ❖ 60 grams onion, chopped
- ❖ 720 millilitres chicken broth
- ❖ 5 grams green onion, sliced
- ❖ 15 millilitres apple cider vinegar
- ❖ 285 grams long-grain brown rice
- ❖ Salt and ground black pepper, as required
- ❖ 45 grams dried cherries

Directions:

1. In a non-stick skillet, melt butter over medium-high and sauté the onions for about 5 minutes.
2. Add the rice and sauté for about 1 minute.
3. Transfer the mixture to a slow cooker.
4. Add the chicken broth, salt, and black pepper and stir to combine.
5. Set the slow cooker on "High" and cook, covered for 3 hours.
6. Uncover the slow cooker and stir in the cherries.
7. Immediately cover the slow cooker or at least 15 minutes.
8. Stir in the green onions and vinegar and serve.

Rice & Veggies Pilaf

Servings|6   Time|2 hours 25 minutes

Nutritional Content (per serving):

Cal| 378   Fat| 10.8g   Protein| 11.6g   Carbs| 57.9g

Ingredients:

- 35 millilitres olive oil
- 1 onion, chopped finely
- 5 grams Greek seasoning
- 790 millilitres vegetable broth
- 2 capsicums, seeded and chopped
- 110 grams feta cheese, crumbled
- Salt and ground black pepper, as required
- 400 grams converted rice
- 10 grams garlic, minced
- 5 grams dried oregano
- 170 millilitres water
- 135 grams olives, pitted and sliced
- 30 millilitres fresh lemon juice

Directions:

1. In a large heavy-bottomed skillet, heat 30 millilitres of the oil over medium heat and sauté the rice for about 2-3 minutes or until browned.
2. Transfer the browned rice into a slow cooker.
3. In the same skillet, heat the remaining oil over medium heat and sauté the onions, garlic, Greek seasoning and oregano for about 4-5 minutes.
4. Transfer the onion mixture into the slow cooker with the broth and water.
5. Set the slow cooker on "High" and cook, covered for 1½ hours.
6. Uncover the slow cooker and stir in the capsicums.
7. Set the slow cooker on "High" and cook, covered for 15 minutes.
8. Uncover the slow cooker and stir in the olives and feta.
9. Set the slow cooker on "High" and cook, covered for 15 minutes.
10. Uncover the slow cooker and stir in the lemon juice, salt and black pepper.
11. Garnish with green onion and serve.

Rice & Beans Pilaf

Servings|8   Time|18½ hours

Nutritional Content (per serving):

Cal| 354   Fat| 16.4g   Protein| 10.8g   Carbs| 44.5g

Ingredients:

- 175 grams dried red beans, soaked overnight and drained
- 270 grams long-grain basmati rice, rinsed
- 500 millilitres unsweetened full-fat coconut milk
- 2½ grams ground ginger
- Salt, as required

- 3 green onions (white and green parts separated), sliced
- 2 garlic cloves, minced
- 720 millilitres vegetable broth
- 30 millilitres fresh lime juice
- 5 grams fresh thyme leaves
- 5 grams ground allspice

Directions:

1. In a large pan of water, add the beans over medium heat and bring to a boil.
2. Cook for about 10-15 minutes.
3. Drain the beans and place into a slow cooker.
4. Add white parts of green onions and remaining ingredients and stir to combine.
5. Set the slow cooker on "Low" and cook, covered for 6-8 hours.
6. Serve immediately with the garnishing of green parts of the green onion.

Rice & Lamb Pilaf

Servings|4   Time|4 hours 20 minutes

Nutritional Content (per serving):

Cal| 424   Fat| 21.2g   Protein| 42g   Carbs| 17.7g

Ingredients:

- ❖ 15 millilitres olive oil
- ❖ 2 medium onions, sliced thinly
- ❖ 130 grams dried apricots
- ❖ 10 grams curry powder
- ❖ 5 grams ground cinnamon
- ❖ Salt and ground black pepper, as required
- ❖ 500 grams boneless lamb shoulder, chopped
- ❖ 1 (400-gram) can diced tomatoes
- ❖ 2 cloves garlic, minced
- ❖ 600 millilitres hot chicken broth
- ❖ 40 grams pine nuts
- ❖ 10 grams fresh mint, chopped

Directions:

1. In a skillet, heat oil over medium-high heat and sear the lamb pieces and oil for about 4-5 minutes.
2. Transfer the lamb mixture into a slow cooker.
3. Add the remaining ingredients except for pine nuts and mint and stir to combine.
4. Set the slow cooker on "Low" and cook, covered for 4 hours.
5. Uncover the slow cooker and stir in the pine nuts and mint.
6. Serve hot.

Rice & Shrimp Pilaf

Servings|4   Time|2½ hours

Nutritional Content (per serving):

Cal| 266   Fat| 2.4g   Protein| 23.1g   Carbs| 36.7g

Ingredients:

- 340 grams frozen shrimp, thawed
- 5 grams red chili powder
- 400 grams cooked rice
- Salt and ground black pepper, as required
- 120 millilitres chicken broth
- 2½ grams dried oregano
- 2½ grams garlic powder
- 145 grams frozen peas, thawed
- 100 grams tomatoes, chopped

Directions:

1. In a lightly greased slow cooker, place the shrimp and top with broth.
2. Sprinkle with the oregano, chili powder and garlic powder.
3. Set the slow cooker on "Low" and cook, covered for 2 hours.
4. Uncover the slow cooker and stir in the rice, peas and tomatoes.
5. Set the slow cooker on "High" and cook, covered for 10-15 minutes.
6. Uncover the slow cooker and stir in the salt and black pepper.
7. Serve hot.

Wild Rice & Mushroom Pilaf

Servings|6   Time|5½ hours

Nutritional Content (per serving):

Cal| 272   Fat| 7.5g   Protein| 12.4g   Carbs| 40.7g

Ingredients:

- ❖ 295 grams wild rice
- ❖ 25 grams green onions, chopped
- ❖ 15 grams butter, melted
- ❖ Salt and ground black pepper, as required
- ❖ 50 grams almonds, chopped
- ❖ 1 (115-gram) can sliced mushrooms with liquid
- ❖ 2 (395- millilitre) cans vegetable broth
- ❖ 40 grams dried cranberries

Directions:

1. In a slow cooker, mix together all ingredients except for cranberries and almonds.
2. Set the slow cooker on "Low" and cook, covered for 4-5 hours.
3. Uncover the slow cooker and immediately stir in cranberries and almonds.
4. Set the slow cooker on "Low" and cook, covered for 15 minutes.
5. Serve warm.

Wild Rice & Corn Pilaf

Servings|6   Time|4¼ hours

Nutritional Content (per serving):

Cal| 238   Fat| 10.9g   Protein| 6.9g   Carbs| 32.1g

Ingredients:

- 15 millilitres olive oil
- 2 cloves garlic, minced
- 150 grams uncooked wild rice blend, rinsed and drained
- Salt and ground black pepper, as required
- 40 grams fresh basil, chopped
- 2 medium onions, chopped
- 2 large capsicums, seeded and chopped
- 125 grams frozen whole kernel corn
- 65 grams pecans, toasted and chopped

Directions:

1. In a large skillet, heat the oil over medium heat and sauté onions and garlic for about 5 minutes.
2. Transfer the onion mixture into a greased slow cooker.
3. Add the remaining ingredients except for pecans and basil and stir to combine.
4. Set the slow cooker on "Low" and cook, covered for 3½-4 hours.
5. Uncover the slow cooker and immediately stir in almonds and basil.
6. Serve warm.

Wild Rice & Chicken Pilaf

Servings|8   Time|4 hours 25 minutes

Nutritional Content (per serving):

Cal| 439   Fat| 21.9g   Protein| 28.4g   Carbs| 32.3g

Ingredients:

- ❖ 295 grams wild rice blend
- ❖ 100 grams wild mushrooms, torn
- ❖ 30 millilitres fresh lemon juice
- ❖ Salt and ground black pepper, as required
- ❖ 910 grams bone-in chicken thighs
- ❖ 4 shallots, halved
- ❖ 5 grams fresh sage, chopped

- ❖ 1 carrot, peeled and chopped
- ❖ 720 millilitres chicken broth
- ❖ 10 grams dried parsley
- ❖ 30 millilitres olive oil
- ❖ 10 grams thyme leaves
- ❖ 5 grams fresh rosemary, chopped

Directions:

1. In a slow cooker, combine the wild rice, carrots, mushrooms, broth, lemon juice, parsley, salt and black pepper.
2. Rub the chicken with 15 millilitres olive oil, thyme, sage, and a pinch of salt and pepper.
3. In a large skillet, heat the remaining olive oil over medium high heat and sear the chicken for about 5 minutes per side.
4. Add in the shallots and cook for about 5-6 minutes.
5. Remove the chicken mixture and place into the slow cooker, skin side up.
6. Sprinkle with the rosemary.
7. Set the slow cooker on "Low" and cook, covered for 3½-4 hours.
8. Serve warm.

Oat & Sausage Pilaf

Servings|6   Time|9 hours 20 minutes

Nutritional Content (per serving):

Cal| 463   Fat| 28g   Protein| 26.7g   Carbs| 23.9g

Ingredients:

- 15 grams butter
- 200 grams steel-cut oats
- Salt and ground black pepper, as required
- 455 grams pork sausage
- 2040 millilitres chicken broth
- 5 grams garlic powder

Directions:

1. In a skillet, melt butter over medium heat and cook sausage for about 10 minutes or until browned.
2. Remove from heat and then cut the sausage links into ½-inch slices.
3. In a slow cooker, add cooked sausage and remaining ingredients and stir to combine.
4. Set the slow cooker on "Low" and cook, covered for 8-9 hours.
5. Serve hot.

Quinoa & Spinach Pilaf

Servings|4   Time|2 hours 40 minutes

Nutritional Content (per serving):

Cal| 286   Fat| 10.9g   Protein| 10.7g   Carbs| 37.6g

Ingredients:

- ❖ 30 millilitres olive oil
- ❖ 480 millilitres vegetable broth
- ❖ 190 grams quinoa, rinsed
- ❖ Salt and ground black pepper, as required
- ❖ 1 onion, chopped
- ❖ 2 large tomatoes, seeded and chopped
- ❖ 60 grams fresh baby spinach

Directions:

1. In a skillet, heat oil over medium heat and sauté onion for about 4-5 minutes.
2. Add broth and tomatoes and bring to a boil.
3. Immediately transfer the tomato mixture into a slow cooker.
4. Add quinoa and black pepper and stir to combine.
5. Set the slow cooker on "Low" and cook, covered for 2 hours.
6. Uncover the slow cooker and stir in spinach.
7. Set the slow cooker on "Low" and cook, covered for 15 minutes.
8. Serve hot.

Vegetarian Recipes

Cheesy Spinach

Servings|5　Time|1 hour 10 minutes

Nutritional Content (per serving):

Cal| 171　Fat| 13.8g　Protein| 9.5g　Carbs| 4g

Ingredients:

- ❖ 85 grams cream cheese, softened
- ❖ Salt and ground black pepper, as required
- ❖ 455 grams fresh baby spinach
- ❖ 115 grams cheddar cheese, shredded

Directions:

1. In a slow cooker, place the cream cheese and top with spinach, followed by cheddar cheese.
2. Set the slow cooker on "High" and cook, covered for 1 hour.
3. Uncover the slow cooker and stir in salt and black pepper.
4. Serve hot.

Broccoli in Cheese Sauce

Servings|6   Time|7¼ hours

Nutritional Content (per serving):

Cal| 159   Fat| 8,2g   Protein| 10.6g   Carbs| 13.1g

Ingredients:

- ❖ 360 grams broccoli florets
- ❖ 5 grams rosemary, minced
- ❖ 525 grams tomato sauce
- ❖ Salt and ground black pepper, as required
- ❖ 1 large onion, chopped
- ❖ 165 grams Swiss cheese, torn
- ❖ 15 millilitres fresh lemon juice

Directions:

1. In a slow cooker, place all ingredients and mix well.
2. Set the slow cooker on "Low" and cook, covered for
3. Cover and cook for about 6-7 hours.
4. Serve hot.

Garlicky Mushrooms

Servings|4   Time|3 hours 10 minutes

Nutritional Content (per serving):

Cal| 30   Fat| 0.4g   Protein| 3.9g   Carbs| 4.8g

Ingredients:

- ❖ 455 grams white button mushrooms, quartered
- ❖ Salt and ground black pepper, as required
- ❖ 3 garlic cloves, minced
- ❖ 20 grams parsley, chopped

Directions:

1. Grease a slow cooker.
2. In the prepared slow cooker, add all ingredients and stir to combine.
3. Set the slow cooker on "High" and cook, covered for 2-3 hours.
4. Serve hot.

Spiced Brinjal

Servings|3   Time|3 hours 10 minutes

Nutritional Content (per serving):

Cal| 129   Fat| 5.7g   Protein| 3.4g   Carbs| 19.9g

Ingredients:

- ❖ 10 millilitres olive oil
- ❖ 1 small tomato, chopped
- ❖ 2½ grams ground cumin
- ❖ 2½ grams ground turmeric
- ❖ 1 medium brinjal, cubed
- ❖ 1 small onion, chopped finely
- ❖ 2½ grams ground coriander

Directions:

1. In a slow cooker, mix together all ingredients.
2. Set the slow cooker on "Low" and cook, covered for 2-3 hours.
3. Serve hot with the garnishing of coriander.

Sweet & Sour Brussels Sprout

Servings|6   Time|4 hours 20 minutes

Nutritional Content (per serving):

Cal| 16   Fat| 9.9g   Protein| 6.5g   Carbs| 17g

Ingredients:

- ❖ 120 millilitres balsamic vinegar
- ❖ 910 grams Brussels sprouts, trimmed and halved
- ❖ 30 grams butter, cubed
- ❖ 30 grams Parmesan cheese, shredded
- ❖ 20 grams brown sugar
- ❖ 30 millilitres olive oil
- ❖ Salt and ground black pepper, as required

Directions:

1. For balsamic reduction: in a small pan, add the vinegar and brown sugar over medium heat and bring to a gentle boil.
2. Cook for about 6-8 minutes, stirring frequently.
3. Remove from the heat and set aside to cool.
4. In a slow cooker, place the Brussels sprouts, olive oil, salt and black pepper, and stir to combine.
5. Place the butter cubes on top.
6. Set the slow cooker on "Low" and cook, covered for 3-4 hours.
7. Uncover the slow cooker and transfer the Brussels sprouts into a bowl.
8. Drizzle with balsamic reduction and serve immediately with the topping of Parmesan.

Butternut Squash with Fruit

Servings|8   Time|4¼ hours

Nutritional Content (per serving):

Cal| 131   Fat| 0.4g   Protein| 2.1g   Carbs| 34.1g

Ingredients:

- ❖ 3 apples, peeled, cored and chopped
- ❖ 60 grams dried cranberries
- ❖ ½ of onion, chopped
- ❖ Salt and ground black pepper, as required
- ❖ 1 (1365 grams) butternut squash, peeled, seeded and cubed
- ❖ 2½ grams garlic powder
- ❖ 10 grams ground cinnamon

Directions:

1. In a slow cooker, mix together all ingredients.
2. Set the slow cooker on "High" and cook, covered for 4 hours.
3. Serve hot.

Mushroom Stroganoff

Servings|3   Time|5 hours 10 minutes

Nutritional Content (per serving):

Cal| 103   Fat| 2.7g   Protein| 10.2g   Carbs| 14.7g

Ingredients:

- 680 grams fresh mushrooms, halved
- 10 grams paprika
- 15 grams sour cream
- 20 grams fresh parsley, chopped
- 1 onion, sliced thinly
- 3 garlic cloves, minced
- 240 millilitres vegetable broth
- Salt and ground black pepper, as required

Directions:

1. In a slow cooker, place the mushrooms, onion, garlic, paprika and broth and stir to combine.
2. Set the slow cooker on "High" and cook, covered for 4 hours.
3. Uncover the slow cooker and stir in the sour cream, salt and black pepper.
4. Serve with the garnishing of parsley.

Ratatouille

Servings|8   Time|8¼ hours

Nutritional Content (per serving):

Cal| 125   Fat| 8.9g   Protein| 2.7g   Carbs| 11.5g

Ingredients:

- 50 grams fresh basil
- 90 millilitres olive oil
- 30 millilitres fresh lemon juice
- Salt, as required
- 2 medium summer squash, cut into small chunks
- 1 large onion, cut into small chunks
- 3 garlic cloves, minced
- 30 millilitres white wine vinegar
- 40 grams tomato paste
- 2 medium courgette, cut into small chunks
- 1 small brinjal, cut into small chunks
- 300 grams cherry tomatoes

Directions:

1. In a food processor, add the basil, garlic, oil, vinegar, lemon juice, tomato paste and salt and pulse until smooth.
2. In the bottom of a slow cooker, place all the vegetables and top with the pureed mixture evenly.
3. Set the slow cooker on "Low" and cook, covered for 5-6 hours.
4. Serve hot.

Mixed Veggie Combo

Servings|4   Time|3¼ hours

Nutritional Content (per serving):

Cal| 203   Fat| 19.3g   Protein| 8.1g   Carbs| 23.6g

Ingredients:

- 15 millilitres olive oil
- 1 small courgette, chopped
- 1 small yellow squash, chopped
- 1 small yellow capsicum, seeded and chopped
- 4 plum tomatoes, chopped
- 10 grams dried basil
- 115 grams feta cheese, crumbled
- 455 grams brinjal, peeled and cut into 1-inch cubes
- 1 small orange capsicum, seeded and chopped
- 1 large onion, chopped
- 4 garlic cloves, minced
- Salt and ground black pepper, as required

Directions:

1. In a slow cooker, place all the ingredients except for cheese and stir to combine.
2. Set the slow cooker on "High" and cook, covered for 3 hours.
3. Serve hot with the topping of feta cheese.

Stuffed Capsicums

Servings|4   Time|4 hours 20 minutes

Nutritional Content (per serving):

Cal| 539   Fat| 20.1g   Protein| 20.5g   Carbs| 64.1g

Ingredients:

- ❖ 4 large capsicums
- ❖ 1 onion, chopped
- ❖ 10 grams garlic, minced
- ❖ 185 grams cooked quinoa
- ❖ 1½ (425-gram) cans black beans, drained
- ❖ 2½ grams ground cumin
- ❖ 15 millilitres olive oil
- ❖ 170 grams cheddar cheese, divided
- ❖ 260 grams jarred tomato salsa
- ❖ 10 grams parsley, minced
- ❖ 2½ grams cayenne pepper

Directions:

1. Remove the stems of bell peppers. Cut about ½-inch of tops of each bell pepper and then chop them.
2. Remove the seeds from inside to create a cup.
3. In a skillet, heat oil over medium heat and sauté onion, garlic and chopped bell pepper tops for about 4-5 minutes.
4. Transfer the onion mixture into a large bowl.
5. Add about 110 grams of cheese and remaining ingredients and stir to combine.
6. Stuff the bell peppers with cheese mixture.
7. In the bottom of a slow cooker, add 90 millilitres of water.
8. Arrange bell peppers in the bottom.
9. Set the slow cooker on "High" and cook, covered for 3-4 hours.
10. Uncover the slow cooker and top each bell pepper with remaining cheese evenly.
11. Cover and cook for about 5 minutes.
12. Serve hot.

Tofu with Broccoli

Servings|4   Time|4 hours 32 minutes

Nutritional Content (per serving):

Cal| 316   Fat| 16.6g   Protein| 19.2g   Carbs| 30g

Ingredients:

- 30 millilitres olive oil
- 1 small onion, chopped
- 10 grams fresh ginger, minced
- 1 (225-gram) can tomato sauce
- 20 grams mustard
- Salt and ground black pepper, as required
- 700 grams small broccoli florets
- 1 (455-gram) package extra-firm tofu, pressed, drained and cubed
- 3 garlic cloves, minced
- 60 millilitres hoisin sauce
- 2½ gams red pepper flakes, crushed
- 30 millilitres water

Directions:

1. For tofu: in a large skillet, heat oil over medium heat and stir fry tofu for about 2 minutes per side.
2. Transfer the tofu into a bowl.
3. In the same skillet, add onion and sauté for about 3-4 minutes.
4. Add ginger and garlic and sauté for 1 minute more.
5. Add remaining ingredients and stir to combine.
6. Cook for about 2-3 minutes, stirring frequently.
7. Add the tofu and sauce mixture into a greased slow cooker and stir to combine.
8. Set the slow cooker on "High" and cook, covered for 3 hours.
9. Uncover the slow cooker and stir in broccoli.
10. Set the slow cooker on "High" and cook, covered for 1 hour.
11. Serve hot.

Spiced Chickpeas

Servings|6   Time|10 hours 20 minutes

Nutritional Content (per serving):

Cal| 239   Fat| 4.8g   Protein| 9.5g   Carbs| 41.7g

Ingredients:

- ❖ 15 grams butter
- ❖ 5 grams ginger, minced
- ❖ 2 jalapeño peppers, chopped
- ❖ 10 grams paprika
- ❖ 5 grams ground turmeric
- ❖ 850 grams canned chickpeas, drained and rinsed
- ❖ Salt and ground black pepper, as required

- ❖ 2 medium onions, chopped
- ❖ 2 garlic cloves, minced
- ❖ 10 grams ground cumin
- ❖ 5 grams ground coriander
- ❖ 1 (395-gram) can diced tomatoes with liquid
- ❖ 170 millilitres vegetable broth
- ❖ 30 millilitres fresh lemon juice
- ❖ 10 grams coriander, chopped

Directions:

1. In a large skillet, melt butter over medium heat and sauté onion for about 8-9 minutes.
2. Add ginger, garlic, jalapeño peppers and spices and sauté for 1 minute more.
3. Add tomatoes with liquid and stir to combine.
4. Now transfer the mixture into a slow cooker.
5. Add remaining ingredients except for lemon juice and coriander and stir to combine.
6. Set the slow cooker on "Low" and cook, covered for 6 hours.
7. Uncover the slow cooker and stir in lemon juice.
8. Serve hot with the garnishing of coriander.

Spiced Lentils

Servings|0   Time|6 hours 10 minutes

Nutritional Content (per serving):

Cal| 290   Fat| 1.0g   Protein| 19.8g   Carbs| 49.8g

Ingredients:

- ❖ 420 grams split red lentils, rinsed
- ❖ 1 medium onion, chopped
- ❖ 10 grams fresh ginger, grated finely
- ❖ 5 grams whole mustard seeds, toasted
- ❖ 5 grams ground turmeric
- ❖ 20 grams fresh coriander leaves, chopped
- ❖ 1200 millilitres water
- ❖ 1 (425-gram) can diced tomatoes
- ❖ 10 grams whole cumin seeds, toasted
- ❖ 5 grams whole fennel seeds, toasted
- ❖ Salt and ground black pepper, as required

Directions:

1. In a slow cooker, add all ingredients except for coriander and stir to combine.
2. Set the slow cooker on "Low" and cook, covered for 4-6 hours.
3. Serve hot with the garnishing of coriander.

Lentil Sloppy Joes

Servings|8   Time|8¼ hours

Nutritional Content (per serving):

Cal| 338   Fat| 3.7g   Protein| 17.4g   Carbs| 61g

Ingredients:

- ❖ 210 grams dried green lentils
- ❖ 1 onion, chopped
- ❖ 1 (425-gram) can salt-free diced tomatoes
- ❖ 5 grams dried oregano, crushed
- ❖ 15 grams red chili powder
- ❖ Salt and ground black pepper, as required
- ❖ 8 whole wheat burger buns
- ❖ ½ of green capsicum, seeded and chopped
- ❖ 75 grams tomato paste
- ❖ 10 grams dried parsley, crushed
- ❖ 10 grams garlic powder
- ❖ 1½ grams cayenne pepper
- ❖ 15 millilitres fresh lemon juice
- ❖ 360 millilitres vegetable broth

Directions:

1. In a slow cooker add all ingredients except for buns and stir to combine.
2. Set the slow cooker on "Low" and cook, covered for 7-8 hours.
3. Serve the lentil mixture in buns.

Quinoa, Chickpeas & Veggie Combo

Servings|6   Time|4¼ hours

Nutritional Content (per serving):

Cal| 537   Fat| 16.1g   Protein| 23.2g   Carbs| 78.5g

Ingredients:

- 600 millilitres unsalted vegetable broth
- 120 grams onions, sliced
- 2 garlic cloves, minced
- Salt, as required
- 75 grams roasted red capsicums, drained and chopped
- 55 grams feta cheese, crumbled
- 10 grams oregano, chopped
- 285 grams quinoa, rinsed
- 1 (440-gram) can chickpeas, drained and rinsed
- 40 millilitres olive oil
- 10 millilitres fresh lemon juice
- 120 grams fresh baby arugula
- 12 kalamata olives, pitted and halved lengthwise

Directions:

1. In a slow cooker, place the broth, quinoa, chickpeas, onions, garlic, 5 millilitres of the oil and salt and stir to combine.
2. Set the slow cooker on "Low" and cook, covered for 3-4 hours.
3. Meanwhile, in a bowl, add the lemon juice, remaining oil and some salt and mix well.
4. Uncover the slow cooker and with a fork, fluff the quinoa mixture.
5. In the slow cooker, add the olive oil mixture, bell peppers and arugula and gently stir to combine.
6. Cover the pot for about 5 minutes before serving.
7. Garnish with olives, feta cheese and oregano and serve.

Beans & Quinoa Chili

Servings|6   Time|6 hours 20 minutes

Nutritional Content (per serving):

Cal| 397   Fat| 11.5g   Protein| 17.1g   Carbs| 60.6g

Ingredients:

- 15 millilitres olive oil
- 2 celery stalks, chopped
- 60 millilitres water
- 10 grams red chili powder
- 5 grams ground coriander
- 2½ grams ground cinnamon
- Pinch of cayenne pepper
- 190 grams quinoa, rinsed
- 1 (425-gram) can fire-roasted, diced tomatoes with juice
- 1 large onion, chopped
- 3 garlic cloves, chopped
- 20 grams chipotle in adobo, chopped finely
- 5 grams ground cumin
- 2½ grams paprika
- 515 grams cooked black beans
- 455grams butternut squash, peeled and cubed
- 1 small avocado, peeled, pitted and sliced

Directions:

1. In a skillet, heat the oil over medium heat and sauté the onion and celery and cook for about 5-7 minutes.
2. Add the garlic and cook for about 1 minute.
3. Add the water, tomato paste, chipotle and spices and cook for about 1 minute, stirring continuously.
4. Transfer the onion mixture into a slow cooker.
5. Add the broth, black beans, quinoa, squash and tomatoes with juice.
6. Set the slow cooker on "Low" and cook, covered for 6 hours.
7. Serve hot with the topping of avocado slices.

Two Beans Chili

Servings|8   Time|8¼ hours

Nutritional Content (per serving):

Cal| 277   Fat| 3.4g   Protein| 17.5g   Carbs| 46.8g

Ingredients:

- ❖ 2 (425-gram) cans black beans, rinsed and drained
- ❖ 2 (400-gram) cans diced tomatoes with juices
- ❖ 2 jalapeño peppers, seeded and chopped
- ❖ 10 grams red chili powder
- ❖ 10 grams ground cumin
- ❖ 1 (425-gram) can pinto beans, rinsed and drained
- ❖ 120 grams onion, chopped
- ❖ 2 garlic cloves, minced
- ❖ 300 millilitres vegetable broth
- ❖ 10 millilitres Worcestershire sauce
- ❖ 55 grams feta cheese, crumbled

Directions:

1. In a slow cooker, add all ingredients except cheese and stir to combine.
2. Set the slow cooker on "Low" and cook, covered for 8 hours.
3. Serve hot with the topping of feta cheese.

Mac n' Cheese

Servings|6   Time|2 hours 10 minutes

Nutritional Content (per serving):

Cal| 237   Fat| 11.7g   Protein| 14.7g   Carbs| 19.4g

Ingredients:

- ❖ 2 egg whites
- ❖ 5 grams tapioca starch
- ❖ 115-grams cheddar cheese, shredded
- ❖ 360 millilitres whole milk
- ❖ 200 grams uncooked whole-wheat macaroni

Directions:

1. In a bowl, add egg whites, milk and tapioca starch and beat until well combined.
2. Add remaining ingredients and stir to combine.
3. Transfer the pasta mixture in a slow cooker.
4. Set the slow cooker on "Low" and cook, covered for 1½-2 hours.
5. Serve hot.

Artichoke Pasta

Servings|4   Time|8¼ hours

Nutritional Content (per serving):

Cal| 479   Fat| 10.4g   Protein| 20.8g   Carbs| 82.2g

Ingredients:

- ❖ 3 (400-gram) cans diced tomatoes
- ❖ 6 garlic cloves, minced
- ❖ 340 grams dried fettuccine pasta
- ❖ 30 grams feta cheese, crumbled
- ❖ 2 (395-gram) cans artichoke hearts, drained and quartered
- ❖ 120 grams whipping cream
- ❖ 50 grams pimiento-stuffed green olives

Directions:

1. Drain the juices from two of the cans of diced tomatoes.
2. In a greased slow cooker, place the drained and undrained tomatoes alongside the artichoke hearts and garlic and mix well.
3. Set the slow cooker on "Low" and cook, covered for 6-8 hours.
4. Meanwhile, in a large pan of the salted boiling water, cook the pasta for about 8-10 minutes or according to the package's directions.Drain the pasta and rinse under cold running water.
5. Uncover the slow cooker and stir in the whipping cream.
6. Divide the pasta onto serving plates and top with artichoke sauce.
7. Garnish with olives and cheese and serve.

Veggie Lasagna

Servings|8   Time|2¼ hours

Nutritional Content (per serving):

Cal| 289   Fat| 8.4g   Protein| 18.8g   Carbs| 37.1g

Ingredients:

- ❖ 1 (140-g) package baby spinach, chopped roughly
- ❖ 1 small courgette, quartered lengthwise and sliced thinly
- ❖ 1 large egg
- ❖ 1 (790-gram) can diced tomatoes
- ❖ 3 garlic cloves, minced
- ❖ 230 grams mozzarella cheese, shredded and divided

- ❖ 3 large Portobello mushrooms, halved and sliced thinly
- ❖ 1 (455-gram) container part-skim ricotta cheese
- ❖ 1 (790-gram) can crushed tomatoes
- ❖ 15 uncooked whole-wheat lasagna noodles
- ❖ Pinch of red pepper flakes

Directions:

1. In a large bowl, add the spinach, courgette, ricotta cheese and egg and mix well.
2. In another bowl, add the tomatoes with juice, garlic and red pepper flakes and mix well.
3. In the bottom of a generously greased slow cooker, place about ¼ of the tomato mixture evenly.
4. Place 5 lasagna noodles over the tomato mixture, overlapping them slightly and breaking them to fit in the pot.
5. Spread half of the ricotta mixture over the noodles.
6. Now, place ¼ of the tomato mixture and sprinkle with 110 grams of mozzarella. Repeat the layers twice.
7. Set the slow cooker on "High" and cook, covered for about 2 hours.
8. Uncover the slow cooker and sprinkle with the remaining mozzarella cheese.
9. Immediately cover the cooker for about 10 minutes before serving.

Index

A

all-purpose flour, 41
allspice, 17, 88
almond milk, 14, 38
almonds, 91, 92
apple, 42, 86
apple cider vinegar, 42, 86
applesauce, 9
artichoke, 34, 57, 115
arugula, 111
asparagus, 77
avocado, 112

B

bacon, 29, 67, 82
balsamic vinegar, 41, 55, 101
barley, 18
basil, 8, 9, 12, 46, 48, 51, 55, 56, 57, 58, 71, 72, 73, 92, 104, 105
bay leaf, 8, 25, 34, 57
beef broth, 26, 38, 39, 40, 57, 61, 63, 64
beef stew meat, 39, 40, 57, 61, 62
black beans, 36, 106, 112, 113
black pepper, 8, 9, 11, 12, 13, 14, 15, 16, 17, 18, 19, 21, 23, 24, 25, 26, 27, 28, 29, 30, 32, 33, 34, 35, 36, 37, 38, 39, 40, 42, 43, 44, 45, 46, 47, 48, 49, 50, 51, 54, 55, 56, 58, 59, 61, 62, 63, 64, 65, 66, 67, 69, 70, 71, 72, 73, 75, 76, 77, 78, 81, 83, 85, 86, 87, 89, 90, 91, 92, 93, 94, 95, 97, 98, 99, 101, 102, 103, 105, 107, 108, 109, 110
boneless beef, 25, 38
boneless pork, 41, 64
brinjal, 32, 100, 104, 105
broccoli, 11, 66, 98, 107
brown rice, 22, 86
Brussels sprouts, 101
burger buns, 110
butter, 8, 11, 43, 46, 58, 59, 76, 77, 79, 80, 81, 83, 84, 85, 86, 91, 94, 101, 108
butternut squash, 14, 37, 102, 112

C

cabbage, 13, 39, 42
cannellini beans, 55
capsicum, 15, 27, 32, 34, 48, 55, 67, 71, 72, 73, 105, 110
carrot, 14, 16, 26, 29, 30, 33, 34, 46, 93

D

cauliflower, 12, 19, 53, 79
cayenne pepper, 15, 29, 36, 37, 47, 70, 73, 106, 110, 112
celery, 8, 16, 18, 19, 22, 23, 24, 25, 26, 27, 29, 30, 34, 35, 44, 46, 51, 72, 112
celery salt, 51
cheddar cheese, 29, 53, 66, 97, 106, 114
chicken breast, 23, 24, 35
chicken broth, 8, 14, 21, 22, 28, 29, 30, 35, 36, 41, 43, 46, 47, 50, 56, 59, 70, 75, 76, 79, 80, 81, 82, 83, 84, 85, 86, 89, 90, 93, 94
chicken tenderloins, 56
chicken thighs, 58, 93
chickpeas, 33, 34, 47, 54, 108, 111
chipotle in adobo, 112
chives, 32
cinnamon, 19, 41, 42, 62, 68, 89, 102, 112
coconut milk, 8, 17, 22, 29, 65, 67, 72, 88
coconut oil, 48, 67, 68
cod, 49
cooked chicken, 21, 81
coriander, 15, 19, 22, 40, 47, 51, 68, 70, 100, 108, 109, 112
courgette, 16, 26, 48, 55, 85, 104, 105, 116
crab legs, 51
cranberries, 91, 102
cream cheese, 53, 56, 97
cream of chicken soup, 56
cream of mushroom soup, 56
creamed corn, 23
cumin, 15, 19, 38, 47, 57, 68, 100, 106, 108, 109, 112, 113
curry paste, 38, 72
curry powder, 17, 22, 40, 50, 89

D

dill, 67, 70
dried apricots, 68, 89
dried cherries, 86
dried herbs, 18
dried plums, 44
dry beans, 28

E

egg, 26, 65, 66, 67, 114, 116

F

fennel, 25, 49, 50, 109
feta cheese, 41, 55, 87, 105, 111, 113, 115

Printed in Great Britain
by Amazon

15174483R00072